Getting Intimate In The Kitchen

Heather Deranja MA, RDN, LD

ISBN: 978-0-0625984-6-7

Cover and chapter photographs by Intimate Images
Hair and makeup by Lindsay King
Location of photos: Magic Chef Mansion, St. Louis, MO.

TABLE OF CONTENTS

A MOMENT OF GRATITUDE AND SPECIAL THANKS

I have to be honest about how this book came about. I was in an obscure place in my life and I was feeling lonely and consumed with doubt about the direction I had taken over the last decade. I have endured many struggles from the day I set out on my path to change the world one bite at a time and become a registered dietitian. I was determined that I had the ability to make a difference in the way people viewed their health, and I wanted so desperately to spread the word by educating individuals about healthy eating and the connection it has to overall quality of life. The adversities were numerous and I wanted many times to just give up and choose an easier route, however in true Leo fashion I knew that wasn't really an option, and I would persevere with dedication despite the obstacles that continuously appeared in my way.

I thought that once I earned my degrees, completed my internship, passed my boards, and had a "big girl" job, that my world would be glorious and I would live happily ever after. However, what I failed to realize was that the sacrifices I had made along my journey didn't have an impact on just me, but my family and friends suffered consequences as well. I had lost touch with all of my close friends and family along the way, but the ones who suffered the most were my daughters because their mom couldn't be there for them as much as they needed. I wasn't able to do the fun things with my girls that I should have because I was so distracted with working and academia so that I could get where I needed to go and succeed. In the end, I lost touch with all those who loved and supported me unconditionally along my journey, and it was a horrible realization that I had completely isolated myself from all of those who cared about and believed in me from day one.

I was feeling sorry for myself and concluded that this was just another hardship in my life that I was faced with, but wasn't sure if I had the strength to overcome it. I was finally ready to throw the towel in and succumb to failure and then one day I woke up and changed my mind. I was compelled to get off of the couch and go into the kitchen; I lit a candle and said to myself "I'm going to cook something". I used to love to cook, but being that I was living alone and only cooking for myself, I didn't see the purpose anymore. I wasn't prepared for the overwhelming sensation that I experienced as I heated the skillet, heard the food sizzling, smelled the aroma of deliciousness cooking in the pan, and tasted the satisfying creation I had made from the scraps I had available in the kitchen. I started looking forward to my days off where I would make a list of recipes I wanted to create, compile a grocery list, and set out to obtain my supplies, then bring them home, turn on some music, and lose myself to the process of creating delicious food. I found myself purchasing flowers every Friday because it felt good. I had started to settle into a new routine that made me feel alive again, and that's when I realized that cooking had become my form of therapy to help me find myself again and get through yet another difficult time in my life.

My renewed passion for cooking inspired me to create this cookbook to help those who struggle in the kitchen to make a healthy meal for themselves or their families. The purpose of this cookbook is to help guide you in preparing and eating foods that are easy to make, will nourish the body, and improve your overall quality of life.

This cookbook would not be a reality if it weren't for many people believing in the project and assisting me along the way in one way or another.

I want to start by thanking my daughters Hannah and Alyssa for being the two most beautiful and precious treasures I will ever be blessed with. You have both inspired me to lead by example and want to be a better mother and person every day. I decided to go back to school and earn my education because I felt it was an important component in showing you that you can achieve anything you set your mind to despite the adversities that have to be overcome. I know that one day you will understand all of this and why it was so important regardless of how hard the journey was. I hope you both will be able to find your passion in life and let that be your guide to happiness.

To my parents for raising me to believe that anything is possible through hard work and dedication. I was taught to value each and every day and to do my best at helping to make the world a better place for all. I was raised in a home filled with unconditional love, compassion, and support. I would not be where I am if you hadn't believed in me and helped to support me in more ways than less. You picked up the slack with the girls when I wasn't able to give more, and I will be forever grateful for all that you have done for us.

To my grandma for inspiring me to learn how to cook, and helping to teach me not to let the fear of failure keep me from trying in the kitchen. I will forever cherish the moments we shared in the kitchen enjoying hot tea, baking and cooking together while listening to the joyous stories of your youth. You showed me how to nurture the needs of others through cooking delicious food.

To all of my friends and family who have dealt with me being completely submerged in my efforts for the last several years. I appreciate you believing in me and understanding my inability to be present in your lives as often as I would like. Thank you for being the guinea pigs of all my creations and helping to guide me with constructive criticism to improve my skills and perfect each dish. Thank you for listening to me preach and explain why I have selected the ingredients for each recipe and why they matter when it comes to nourishing the body and improving overall health. Most importantly, I want to thank you for always being there when I need you, and I look forward to spending more quality time together relaxing and having fun.

To my clients for helping me to recognize a need for a tool that can be used to educate and motivate others to explore the "dark side" of the kitchen. I appreciate all of your support and encouragement throughout the development of this book. I appreciate your patience with me as I strove to be a perfectionist to offer you the best possible recipes and cookbook I could conjure. A special thanks to all of you who were brave enough to give the recipes a try and provided me with endless positive feedback.

A special thanks to Dr. Jeff Hallazgo for believing in me, seeing something special in "Nutrition Vixen", and knowing that it needed to be shared with the world. I explained the vision I had in my head for what I wanted this cookbook to look like, and you helped make that dream come true and for that I will forever be grateful.

To Intimate Images for capturing the beautiful and timeless images distributed throughout this cookbook. You approached me about doing a pinup shoot and I propositioned you with this project and you executed it beautifully.

To Shelley Donaho for opening up her beautiful home *The Magic Chef Mansion* and allowing us to create the images used in the book to represent the Nutrition Vixen theme.

To Lindsay King for your endless hours spent helping Nutrition Vixen develop multiple components used throughout the cookbook, especially the time spent plugging in ingredients to develop the nutrition facts for each recipe. I'm grateful for your creative eye and nailing my pinup hair and makeup used for the photos in the cookbook. You have a talented gift my friend and you are going to be a valuable dietitian, and I look forward to watching you grow as a professional.

To David Hogan for inspiring me to use my talents in the kitchen and my passion for nutritious food to create the cookbook so others can enjoy the recipes. I appreciate all of the meals you have devoured and the feedback you have given me to perfect each recipe. If it weren't for you hassling me to move to action, I would still be pondering over a logo and website design. I appreciate all of the motivation you have provided me in pursuing my dream.

Last but certainly not least, to Taylor Giacin: the hats you wear are endless. I wouldn't have been able to accomplish this cookbook without your continuous dedication to the cause and believing in the project even when I didn't. You have helped capture all of the spontaneous ideas and visions I have had pertaining to the material in the cookbook, and helped to guide my thought process and format the ideas in a way that can be shared and enjoyed by all. Thank you for being my taste tester and allowing me to violate your food sensitives repeatedly, and for literally indulging in every single recipe in this cookbook multiple times until I perfected each and every one. I appreciate your endless friendship and encouragement to pick myself up and forge forward even on the days I didn't want to: this cookbook wouldn't be a reality if it weren't for you. We have shared and grown so much together throughout this process and I will forever cherish the times we had together making this dream come true. Cinnamon, nutmeg, cloves, and pumpkin everything...flatbread, tapas, clutches, jacket or no jacket! I can't wait to get started on the next cookbook!

MEET THE NUTRITION VIXEN

I'm Heather, better known as the Nutrition Vixen. I am a registered and licensed dietitian nutritionist, weight loss coach, cook, and mother. I achieved a bachelor of science in Dietetics and masters of art in Multidisciplinary Health Communications through Fontbonne University in St. Louis, Missouri. I'm passionate about nutrition and know firsthand the benefits of maintaining a healthy diet and lifestyle to self-manage and reduce symptoms associated with chronic disease.

I was diagnosed with a kidney disease in my late teens and was unable to acquire health insurance which led to my pursuit of knowledge in the field of nutrition to ensure a better quality of life. The standardized, fix-it-with-a-pill approach on which modern medicine is built doesn't take into account the benefits of medical nutrition therapy and this approach contributes to the growing epidemic of chronic disease and diminished quality of life. I decided to become a dietitian to increase awareness of risks and benefits associated with nutrition, provide education, and coach individuals through the process of behavior change that will allow them to take appropriate action to become self-sufficient and obtain a healthier lifestyle.

It seems that everywhere I look these days someone has a self-proclaimed "expert" opinion about diet and nutrition. With that comes an array of misinformation promoting health fraud from sources such as websites, television, radio, magazines, newspapers, advertisements, friends, and family. With the growing evidence that supports the connection between nutrition and overall health, many consumers are becoming more aware that changing their current behaviors can ensure a healthy lifestyle. However, with the multitude of mixed nutrition information available, making nutrition decisions while shopping and eating can be overwhelmingly confusing.

I'm passionate about debunking diet rumors, myths, and fads, while teaching people how to eat foods that are scientifically proven to prevent disease and promote optimal health and wellness. I'm committed to taking research-based information and breaking it down into simple, practical terms that can be implemented into any lifestyle to achieve desired health, fitness, and weight-loss goals. I understand the daily struggles that most people are faced with when it comes to changing nutrition behaviors. My approach is different than most nutritionists because I don't believe in micromanaging food intake by counting calories or points, limiting grams of fat, or following a specific meal plan. Instead I focus on creating practical strategies that support healthy behaviors that are realistic, achievable, and can be sustained by any lifestyle.

GETTING INTIMATE IN THE KITCHEN WITH NUTRITION VIXEN

In my experience as a registered dietitian and working with clients of all ages, I discovered common barriers that were among the majority when it comes to changing nutrition behaviors. I often hear "I don't know how to cook", or "I don't know what to cook", or "I don't know how to take the information and make it into a meal that I can eat". I decided to lead by example and show others that eating healthy didn't have to be complicated and therefore the solution to their problems lies within this cookbook. I wanted to create a resource that is user-friendly and will inspire anyone to get into the kitchen and cook up something nutritious and delicious.

Cooking can seem like a pain in the ass, but that doesn't mean you have to swing by the drive-thru on your way home or heat up a frozen meal. Depending on take-out, drive-thru, or packaged foods on a regular basis can wreak havoc on your health and your waistline in no time. Cooking has many benefits that can help you take charge of your health regardless of your age or culinary skills. You can learn to cook delicious, quick, healthy, and inexpensive meals with a few simple shopping and cooking tips. Therefore, Nutrition Vixen is tempting you to indulge in food the healthy way!

TOXINS: WHY THEY MATTER AND 4 SIMPLE STEPS TO DETOXIFY THE BODY

Let's make it simple, we are all bombarded by toxins day in and day out through the food supply, the water we drink, bathe and swim in, personal hygiene and cosmetic items we use, and the air we breathe. In addition to these external toxins, we also have internal toxins that are created by improper digestion or hormone imbalances.

Our bodies are BEYOND taxed!

Never before has the human body been presented with such a heavy burden of foreign substances to metabolize and eliminate. There are over 80,000 chemicals in use today and only a fraction of them are ever tested for safety! Over 90% of chemical pesticides are found in our food supply alone. In addition, excessive use of fast food, caffeine, and alcohol are prevalent among adults in the US, and don't forget the widespread use of over-the-counter and prescription medications to top it off. All of these components tax the human body beyond its natural capabilities of detoxification.

The formal definition of detoxification is: The process where we convert internal & external toxins into substances that can be removed from our body.

Most toxins are fat soluble or better known as "fat-loving" and seek out our fat and nerve cells, reproductive organs, and the liver to reside. We can't dodge these toxins but when our body is overloaded with toxicity and our natural detoxification organs can't keep up in removing the toxins, problems occur with our health and unexplainable symptoms present themselves.

Toxicity, infection, and hormone imbalances make it impossible to lose weight and feel good. Toxins burn cell membranes, irritate the lining of blood vessels, and damage the mitochondria (power house) of our cells. In order to reduce the risk of health problems like heart disease and cancer from toxin exposure, proactive steps must be taken to eliminate and reduce toxins from the body.

The most common toxins found in the human body include:

Staph	Malonic acid	Pesticides
Aluminum	Mercury	Bacteria
Solvents	Toluene	Fungus/mold
Parasites	Arsenic	Virus
Strep	Lead	Dyes
Chemicals		

The most common warning signs of toxicity include:

Headaches	Insomnia
Fatigue	Immune weakness
Poor concentration	Joint and muscle discomfort
Decreased memory	Weight gain
Constipation	Digestive complaints
Depression	Arthritis
Anxiety	Fibromyalgia

In addition to the symptoms mentioned previously, if you find yourself relating to one or more of the conditions listed below you would definitely benefit from detoxification:

- Chemical sensitivities – this is sensitivity to odors like cologne, perfume, deodorizers, scented candles, etc.
- Sensitivity to or poor tolerance of medications or nutrition supplements
- Thyroid or hormonal issues
- Skin disruptions like eczema, psoriasis, dermatitis, or rashes
- Don't sweat appropriately – when you work out hard or go into the sauna, you don't sweat very much
- Constipation – this is defined as <1 bowel movement a day
- Excess cellulite
- Edema or water retention – may see more around your ankles with sock lines, waist with waist lines, fingers if your rings are tight

Reduce YOUR toxins!

Now that you understand how toxicity affects your health, and perhaps relate to some of the signs and symptoms you might be experiencing, what can you do? You start by eliminating them, in other words…you don't take them in! Here are some simple tips to start reducing the amount of toxins that would otherwise be stored in your body fat.

1. Let's start with the air you breath- We often think of pollution as something only present outside, but the truth is the air inside homes, offices, and other buildings can be just as polluted as the outside air. The air inside your home can be contaminated by lead (in house dust), formaldehyde, fire-retardants, radon, carbon monoxide, volatile chemicals from conventional cleaners, microscopic dust mites, mold and pet dander. It's important to make sure that you change the air filter in your home every three months. Be sure to have routine inspections of the furnace before operating in the fall. Install carbon monoxide detectors inside the home and on each floor if you live in a multiple level home to detect carbon monoxide poisoning. If the home has moisture,

identify the source and properly eliminate it and remove water damaged materials from the home to eliminate harmful mold and dust mites that can create serious health problems. Keep the humidity inside the home around 30%- 50% to help keep allergens under control, and if needed purchase a dehumidifier to reduce moisture. Make your home a smoke-free zone. Cigarette smoke contains over 4,000 chemicals, which is associated with increased risk of multiple health conditions related to breathing in second hand smoke. Finally, eliminate the use of conventional household cleaners and switch to natural/organic household cleaners to decrease exposure to chemicals and toxins that pollute the air quality.

2. Don't drink that water- We know that water is a life sustaining source, however not all water is created equal. Tap water is tainted with toxins that are dangerous to your health, so caution should be taken when drinking and bathing using tap water. Do yourself a favor and invest in a filtration system or at least purchase a filter for your drinking faucets and shower heads to reduce your exposure to harmful toxins. The EPA's lenient standards allow for common toxins like arsenic, boric acid, formaldehyde, pesticides, lead, fluorosilicic acid, and harmful bacteria such as E.coli in the tap water. If that wasn't enough to convince you, harmful pharmaceutical medicines like antibiotics, anti-convulsants, mood stabilizers, and sex hormones are found in the drinking water supply. That's a pretty scary list, so make sure you take action to protect yourself and don't forget to change your filters frequently to ensure good health by reducing exposure to these toxins. In addition, you can check the Toxins Release Inventory (TRI) report for chemicals in your area by visiting the Environmental Protection Agency (EPA) website at www.epa.gov

3. *Stop! Don't eat that*- Food is any substance consumed to provide nutritional support for the body that contains essential nutrients to support health, but some food sources also contain dangerous toxins that can make you sick, fat, and feel like crap. It is difficult to know where to begin because our food supply is so tainted with substances that are harming our health, but let's take a look at some of the issues with conventional products and why we should be concerned:

Deciding to purchase organic food can be a bit confusing and intimidating to your pocket book, so I'm going to clean this up and help you decide what products are worth the added expense associated with "organic" food purchases to protect your health.

What does "organic" mean anyway and why does it matter? The word "organic" applies to any food item that is produced without the use of conventional pesticides, herbicides, fertilizers, and animal products that are raised without the use of hormones and antibiotics. Making sure you purchase the right produce and animal products matters because ultimately, "you are what you eat" and these toxins can wreak havoc on your metabolism and ability to lose weight and keep it off.

Let's start with meat. We are told we need to make protein a priority at all meals and snacks to support our resting metabolism, balance blood sugar, build lean muscle tissue, and support the immune system, however if we are consuming protein sources from conventionally raised animals, it may be doing more harm than good. Conventionally raised animals are fed diets that consist of grains such as soy and corn. The animals ingest the grains that are treated with pesticides, herbicides, fungicides and fertilizers and then stored as toxins in the fat of the animals. The animals that are fed grain diets also have higher Omega-6 levels which contribute to inflammation. When selecting proteins from animals, it's best to purchase pasture-raised, grass-fed, or all natural choices. Look for the organic label to ensure that it's been raised without hormones, antibiotics, and pesticides. When selecting seafood, avoid anything farm raised and choose wild caught. Simply swapping your proteins out for less toxic options will increase your intake of Omega-3 and decrease your toxicity. One thing to note about eating organic meat is that it does not have to cost your whole paycheck. Look for sales at your local grocery store, as well as discounted meats that are close to the sell by date, buy them in bulk and freeze them for later use.

Dairy products should be organic as well for all of the same reasons mentioned above but specifically to reduce exposure to recombinant bovine growth hormone (rBGH) which is a synthetic (man-made) hormone that is marketed to dairy farmers to increase milk production in cows. It has been used in the United States since it was approved by the Food and Drug Administration (FDA) in 1993, but its use is not permitted in the European Union, Canada, Australia, New Zealand, and Japan. Cows treated with the rBGH tend to develop infected udders and are treated heavily with antibiotics to reduce infections. Bovine growth hormone levels are not higher in milk from cows treated with rBGH, however the milk from cows treated with rBGH have another hormone known as insulin-like growth factor (IGF-1) levels that are much higher. This raises concern because the hormone IGF-1 helps some types of cells to grow. Research indicates that levels of high IGF-1 correlate with development of certain tumors, potentially increasing the risk of cancer.

I often refer my clients to cured meats because they are an easy way to add protein to the diet especially when you are on the go. However, cured meats are another area of concern due to the long shelf life and added preservatives. These preservatives know as nitrates and nitrites slow down the breakdown of fats in the package, and unfortunately your body too! So make sure to read the labels and look for "naturally uncured" or "nitrate and nitrite free" varieties of bacon, sausage, deli meats, jerky and smoked salmon. Look for brands that are naturally cured, they taste the same as the artificially cured alternatives but are safer because they use natural ingredients like sea salt and celery juice to preserve the meats.

The Good, Better, and Best: Decoding the Packages of Meat, Dairy, Eggs and Seafood

Beef and Lamb

Baseline: commercial, hormone and antibiotic-free

Good: organic

Better: grass-fed, pasture-raised

Best: 100% grass-fed and finished, pasture-raised, local

Eggs and Poultry

Baseline: commercial

Good: cage-free, organic

Better: free-range, organic

Best: pasture-raised, organic

Pork

Baseline: commercial

Good: organic

Better: free-range, organic

Best: pasture-raised, organic

Dairy

Baseline: commercial or organic

Good: grass-fed

Better: raw/unpasteurized

Best: grass-fed, raw/unpasteurized

Seafood

Baseline: Farm-raised (not recommended)

Good: non-grain fed

Better: wild-caught

Best: wild fish

What Do The Labels Mean?

Pasture-raised: Animals are allowed to roam freely in their natural environment and are able to eat a natural diet that consists of grasses, plants, bugs and grubs.

Free-range: Poultry must have access to the outdoors at least 51% of the time; however, there are no restrictions of what the birds can be fed.

Cage-free: Poultry are uncaged inside barns or warehouses, and generally do not have access to the outdoors.

Naturally raised: United States Department of Agriculture (USDA) verified term. Animals are raised entirely without growth promotants, antibiotics (except for ionophores used as coccidiostats for parasite control) and have never been fed animal by-products.

Organic: Animals raised without the use of hormones or antibiotics unless in the case of illness. Animals are fed an organic diet and have access to the outdoors; however, they are not necessarily grass-fed.

Natural: Products contain no artificial ingredients or added colors and are minimally processed. Minimally processed means that the item has not been processed in a manner that fundamentally alters the product.

No added hormones: the use of hormones is prohibited in the raising of pork and poultry; therefore, this is unnecessary on the package. However, beef and lamb must be raised without the use of hormones to be labeled hormone free.

Wild fish: The fish was spawned, lived in, and was caught in the wild.

Wild caught fish: The fish was caught in the wild; however, that doesn't mean that it was spawned or lived in the wild for the entirety of its life.

Naturally uncured: meat products that have been preserved without the use of sodium nitrate or sodium nitrite.

Sources: For more information please visit www.usda.gov and www.ewg.org

We've all been told an apple a day keeps the doctor away, but if that apple has been treated with pesticides you might want to pass. According to the Centers for Disease Control and Prevention there are traces of 29 different pesticides in the average American's body. The negative health effects of pesticides are numerous and depending on the type of chemical, it can have carcinogenic effects, or may affect hormones and the endocrine system. You can view a full list of the EPA's human health risk assessment of pesticides on their website at www.epa.gov. Produce should make up 50% of the food on your plate, so make sure that you purchase organic produce for the "*dirty dozen*" and choose a variety of items from the "*clean fifteen*".

The Dirty Dozen are the fruits and vegetables that have the highest levels of pesticide residue and are ranked starting with the most toxic to the least toxic. The Clean Fifteen are the fruits and vegetables that are pesticide-free in non-organic form. If you can't afford to purchase organic produce, make sure to wash conventional produce well. You can also soak your fruits and veggies in white wine vinegar to remove any excess toxins. Since most of the toxic residue is sprayed on the surface of conventional produce, don't forget to peel away any skin before you eat it to remove excess toxins. The following chart can be used to help guide you when making decisions about safe food purchases. For more information, check out the Environmental Working Group (EGW) 2015 Shopper's Guide to Pesticides in Produce at www.ewg.org or www.foodnews.org

The *Dirty* Dozen	The *Clean* Fifteen
1. Apples	1. Onions
2. Celery	2. Frozen sweet corn
3. Sweet bell peppers	3. Pineapple
4. Peaches	4. Avocado
5. Strawberries	5. Cabbage
6. Imported nectarines	6. Frozen sweet peas
7. Imported grapes	7. Asparagus
8. Spinach	8. Mangoes
9. Lettuce	9. Eggplant
10. Cucumbers	10. Kiwi
11. Domestic blueberries	11. Cantaloupe
12. Potatoes	12. Sweet potatoes
	13. Watermelon
	14. Grapefruit
	15. Mushrooms

Finally, it's important to note that we need to avoid artificial sweeteners that are not found in nature. Artificial sweeteners such as sucralose (Splenda), aspartame (Equal), saccharin (Sweet 'N Low), cyclamate, alitame, acesulfame-K, and neotame are manmade chemicals used to sweeten products. The problem with these artificial sweeteners is that each one has a different chemical makeup with potentially different side effects; however, they are all derived from known dangerous chemical compounds.

Unfortunately, limited research has been done on these artificial sweeteners to know exactly the extent of danger they present to the human body. So to be safe, avoid artificial sweeteners and use natural sweeteners like honey and raw cane sugar, but remember to use these in moderation because they can have toxic effects on the body as well.

4. Don't forget to sweat- Using the dry sauna can be very helpful in excreting toxins from the body. The infrared light penetrates the skin deeper allowing for the ion bonds of large water molecules to break up into smaller particles, releasing toxins by trapping them into the sweat. Not all toxins are excreted through sweat and some are released into the bloodstream and are eliminated via the liver, kidneys, and bowels. For optimal results, use the dry sauna a minimum of three times a week for 15 minutes or as tolerated. Consult with your physician if you have high blood pressure or are pregnant before using the sauna. It's important to note that you must rinse off immediately after exiting the dry sauna to ensure that the toxins have been removed and are not absorbed back into the bloodstream through the skin.

I hope that you have found this information to be beneficial and that you will start detoxing your body one step at a time. You can take it one step further by following a detoxification program that assists the liver in phase 1 and phase 2 of detoxification to remove harmful toxins trapped in the liver tissue and fat cells of the body.

THE BITTER TRUTH ABOUT SUGAR

It's very easy for consumers to get confused when shopping for "healthier" options to satisfy their sweet tooth. Do you think choosing the cookies sweetened with honey or fruit juice concentrate is a better choice than the option sweetened with white sugar? Unfortunately, sugar is sugar regardless of the alias it hides behind. Food manufacturers are very crafty at disguising sugars used to sweeten popular junk foods and advertise them as healthy alternatives. Consumers are deceived by food labels that make claims such as "no sugar added" or "all natural sugars" but the bottom line is they are all sugar, and have equivalent damaging health consequences. You can use the table below to help familiarize yourself with popular names used to indicate hidden sugars in packaged and processed foods.

Two hundred years ago, the average American consumed only 2 pounds of sugar per year. According to the American Heart Association (AHA), today the average American consumes 156 pounds of added sugar per year- this equals 1 cup per day. High-sugar diets have been linked to numerous health issues, including tooth decay, obesity, increased risk for high blood pressure, high triglyceride levels, and other risk factors for heart disease and stroke. The AHA recommends limiting the amount of added sugar to no more than 100 calories per day for women (6 teaspoons) and 150 calories per day for men (9 teaspoons).

Soft drinks contribute more sugar to the average American diet than any other food. One 12 oz. can of soda has 11 teaspoons of sugar. The average American drinks 20 oz. of soda per day which has 18 teaspoons of sugar. You can use the following formula to keep track of your sugar intake, you might be really surprised how much sugar you actually consume on a daily basis. Here's how you calculate your sugar intake, 4 grams of sugar = 1 teaspoon = 15 calories.

It's important to note that artificial sweeteners are not recommended and naturally derived sweeteners should be used in moderation. It does make a difference when selecting a sweetener to use. The best sweeteners to use are the ones that are the least processed, which include honey (preferably raw, organic, and local), maple syrup, green leaf stevia, or stevia extract and molasses.

Sugar Alias

agave nectar	fruit juice concentrate
Barbados sugar	galactose
barley malt	glucose
beet sugar	glucose solids
blackstrap molasses*	high fructose corn syrup (HFCS)
brown sugar	honey*
buttered syrup	icing sugar
cane juice crystals	invert sugar
cane sugar	lactose
cane-juice crystals	malt
caramel	malt syrup
carob syrup	maltodextrin
confectioner's sugar	maltose
corn sweetener	mannitol
corn syrup	maple syrup*
corn syrup solids	molasses*
date sugar	raw sugar
dextran	refiner's syrup
dextrose	sorbitol
diastatic malt	sorghum syrup
diatase	sucrose
ethyl maltol	sugar
Florida crystals	stevia (green leaf or extract)
fructose	carob powder
fruit juice (real, fresh)	turbinado sugar
	yellow sugar
	xylitol- this is a sugar alcohol

Artificial sweeteners include:
Acesulfame K (*Sweet One*)
Aspartame (*Equal, Nutra-Sweet*)
Saccharin (*Sweet'N Low*)
Stevia: white/bleched (*Truvia, Sun Crystals*)
Sucralose (*Splenda*)
Tagatose

*These sources of sugar are the better options, however use in moderation.

COOKING FOR ONE: STRATEGIES TO GET YOU IN THE KITCHEN

Nowadays, more and more people live alone either by choice or circumstance, including myself, and it can be very difficult to motivate myself to want to cook a meal after a long day of work. However, choosing to be lazy leaves me with limited options that aren't very healthy. The simple solution is to order take-out, hit the drive-thru, or throw a frozen meal in the microwave, but over time these choices add inches to your waistline and increase your risk for chronic disease because these meals are low in nutritional quality and high in unhealthy fats, sugar, sodium, and calories. Keep in mind you are what you eat, so don't be fast, cheap, easy, or fake! The following material contains strategies that will help you to get in the kitchen and make healthy and delicious food, even if it's just for you!

STOP BITCHIN' AND GET IN THE KITCHEN!

Alright, it's time to get off your ass and get in the kitchen to start cooking so you can save money, increase your energy, improve your mood, and your overall health. What? Stop bitching about how you don't know what to do or you don't have the right tools to prepare a meal. Cooking for yourself doesn't mean you have to be a gourmet chef or have all the fancy kitchen gadgets to satisfy your taste buds, you just need a few simple things to make a meal. Don't let fear hold you back from taking control over your diet and health. Too often I hear my clients say, "I don't know how to cook, my family didn't cook, so how am I supposed to do it?" Well, the answer is you try! Yes, you will fail but with each fail you will learn what not to do the next time. Stop being such a biotch! The best part about cooking for one is that you can be selfish and you don't have to please anyone but yourself.

Oh, and one more thing, cooking healthy does not mean you have to spend your whole paycheck to make dinner. When you first start cooking, your initial expenses will be a little higher because you will be investing in some staple items that you will need on hand to cook a badass meal at any time. The tips in this book will help you save money by doing a little planning. Yes, I said it: you are going to have to spend a little time thinking ahead, oh how that sucks! Just remember this: when you fail to plan, you plan to fail!

GETTING BACK TO BASICS

When it comes to changing your eating habits, the transition can be overwhelming especially if you rely on your meals from fast food, take out, or prepackaged foods. I don't recommend eliminating everything at one time; you have to be realistic with changes by simplifying the process and taking it one day at a time. This will ensure you achieve sustainable results in the long run. When you decide to start adding whole foods to your diet, you have to consider what you're willing to commit to each day. Most people think this should be an easy shift, however there is a reason you aren't doing it in the first place. You must make the transition achievable by establishing behavior change goals that are realistic. If you currently aren't eating any vegetables, does adding one serving of vegetables seem doable? Maybe you aren't willing to start making your own meals yet but you can swap out the French fries for a side salad. Allowing yourself to set small goals that you can achieve will help build momentum to keep you going and change more behaviors.

If this is your first rodeo, then we have to approach it with a little caution. I recommend you learn one new culinary skill each week, or if you are ambitious and want to dominate that bull, aim for one per day. If you aren't sure how to cut, chop, or dice things you can start there. There is an abundance of resources available to assist you in acquiring the necessary skills to cook a badass meal. You can search the internet for how-to videos, search cookbooks and blogs, or take a beginner cooking class, or purchase a tool that does it for you...I'm guilty, I must admit I have several tools that I love and use often while cooking to make the job a little easier. Learning some basic skills will increase your confidence when you walk into the ring. The easier and more efficient you become at cooking tasks, the more likely you will be to commit to them daily.

CREATING THE LIST

Creating healthy eating habits starts with a list. Taking the time to write a list of items you need can help you organize your meals which will save you time and money. Think about what you will want to eat for breakfast, lunch, dinner and snacks throughout the week. If this is your first attempt at planning out your meals, aim for 2-3 days instead of trying to tackle the whole week, as that can be a little overwhelming. I use recipes that have few ingredients and use the same spices and seasonings to help reduce grocery expenses.

A FEW MONEY SAVING TIPS

• Incorporate seasonal fresh fruit and vegetables in your meal planning to reduce expenses, and in addition shop for produce every 3-4 days to reduce waste and save money

• Purchase frozen vegetables and fruits with no added sugars or sauces. These are convenient and allow for you to use what you need and save the rest for later

• Purchase block cheese and shred it at home instead of buying shredded cheese. Blocks will last longer and save you money

• Purchase frozen bags of wild-caught fish like salmon and/or antibiotic and hormone free chicken breast that you can package and freeze individually. This will allow you to defrost what you need and save the rest for another time

• Purchase grains, dried beans, flour, and nuts from the bulk section. This will allow you to try new things without committing to a 5 lb. bag. Bulk foods cost less than packaged foods

PREP TIME BASICS

One of the reasons it's so hard to give up the processed foods is because of the convenience factor. Whenever I go grocery shopping I have the greatest intentions of eating healthy by loading up on fresh produce. However, I can't tell you how many times I've gone to the fridge, opened it up and decided that it contained options that were inconvenient and instead I reached for the pita chips and hummus. To overcome this habit, I had to re-train myself and create new habits. Whenever I go grocery shopping I automatically schedule prep time when I get home. I refuse to place any produce in the refrigerator without prepping it first. I mimic the appeal of processed foods by having healthy options that I can just grab and go. Prepping your food will take a little extra time but opening the fridge and seeing berries that are already washed or celery and peppers already cut into strips when you're hungry and reaching for a snack will make a world of difference in selecting a healthy choice. If you are too lazy and can't bring yourself to take the time to wash and cut up produce to be prepared, then you can always purchase produce that is already prepped, however you will pay more for the convenience.

CREATING THE HEALTHY PLATE

Whenever it comes to planning an actual meal, most people overthink it and make it more complicated than it needs to be. All of my recipes are designed using a template to ensure they are nutrient dense meals that will support your metabolism. Choosing any of the recipes in this book as a meal will take the guesswork out and you can be confident that you are eating a nutrient balanced meal that will keep you feeling satisfied for hours. To save time throughout the week, try cooking in batches to help you stay committed to your healthy eating efforts. Cooking a recipe that makes a few servings can be used later in the week as lunch or dinner. You can also freeze leftovers in individual serving sizes and pull them out when you are short on time or just don't feel like cooking.

SET THE SCENE

Food prep and cooking aren't always the most exciting things on my to-do list, however I always approach the task by changing my mindset and making it enjoyable. When I grocery shop I purchase fresh flowers to brighten my mood and my kitchen. Treating yourself to flowers each week is a beautiful thing because you deserve them. I light a candle that smells good to elicit my sense of smell which encourages me to take deep breaths and relax. Finally, I turn on music that fits my mood. Listening to music while I slice and dice helps to make the tasks at hand a little more enjoyable. Just remember, we have the choice to make any task worthwhile and it will be rewarding on many levels. Getting in the kitchen can help strengthen your mind, body, and spirit if you approach it with the right mindset.

I hope these tips have inspired you to get off your ass and into the kitchen! The task of cooking never gets any easier, however the more you do it, the better you get and your confidence will grow and so will your recipe collection. Before you know it you will be hosting your own dinner parties!

PANTRY STAPLES

When it comes to creating healthy and delicious meals, there are a few items I can't do without. My pantry is always stocked with the following items because I want to have everything I need when my cooking creativity strikes! Having these items at all times ensures that I can always whip up a nutritious meal even if I'm crunched for time.

Pantry Item	Health Benefits
Unsweetened, full-fat coconut milk	Good alternative to dairy, excellent source of heart healthy fat, low in sugar
Unsweetened coconut flakes	Good source of fiber, potassium, magnesium, excellent source of heart healthy fat, low in sugar
Coconut oil	Stable for cooking at high temperatures, heart healthy fat
Almond butter (no added sugars, oils, or preservatives)	Good source of monounsaturated fat, protein, fiber, calcium, phosphorous, vitamin E, and magnesium. Perfect snack for stabilizing blood sugars
Grass-fed butter	Contains fat soluble vitamins A, D, E, K. Contains CLA (conjugated linolenic acid), which has anti-cancer properties and helps to assist in weight loss (particularly in the abdomen), only found butter from grass-fed cows
Extra virgin olive oil (unrefined)	High in antioxidants, contains healthy monounsaturated fats
Ground flaxseed	Essential fatty acid, good source of omega-3 from alpha-linolenic acid, good source of fiber, contains cancer fighting lignans which protect against breast and prostate cancer
Chia seeds	Promote satiety keeping you feeling fuller for longer, contain omega-3 fatty acids and antioxidants
Quinoa	High protein seed, gluten free, good source of calcium, phosphorous, magnesium, potassium, copper, manganese, zinc, and iron

Dry beans/Canned beans (rinsed and drained)	High in fiber, stabilize blood sugar, high in antioxidants, excrete toxins form the body
Canned diced tomatoes (no salt added)	Rich in the carotenoid lycopene, which contains many cancer fighting properties. Also high in antioxidants and lutein, which is great for your eyes
Protein powder (non-soy protein powder)	Provides high quality protein, aides in weight loss and lean muscle gain, supports the immune system
Almond flour	Great substitute for traditional flour, gluten free, rich in heart healthy monounsaturated fat, promotes satiety, good source of protein and fiber
Coconut Flour	Great substitute for traditional flour, gluten free, high in fiber and heart healthy fat
Unsweetened cocoa powder and dark chocolate (at least 70% cocoa)	Contains flavanols that reduce the risk of heart attacks and strokes, rich in magnesium
Raw wild honey	Great for adding natural sweetness, rich in flavonoids and antioxidants, provides immune support
Frozen and chopped onions and peppers	Purchase frozen and chopped vegetables for convenience when cooking, saves preparation time
Frozen organic berries	Contain cancer fighting properties, high in antioxidants, memory protecting food
Himalayan pink sea salt	Rich in minerals, can help regulate hydration and pH, far superior to iodized salt because it is free of toxins and chemicals from processing
Roasted red peppers (no added sugars or preservatives)	Excellent source of vitamin C, vitamin A, and potassium. Contain lycopene which has been shown to reduce risk of prostate cancer
Minced garlic	Has been shown to help lower LDL "bad" cholesterol, raise HDL "good" cholesterol, and prevent blood clots. Has anti-cancer properties and contains antioxidants

Stevia extract (no added maltodextrin or lactose)	Natural sweetener derived from a plant, works well as a sugar substitute in baking and cooking
Balsamic vinegar (no added sulfites)	Contains healthy vitamins, minerals, and amino acids. Fights off toxins and bacteria
Ground cumin	Has been shown to reduce allergy symptoms, contain anti-cancer properties, and helps to reduce heartburn and assist in digestion. Good source of iron
Chili powder	Rich in nutrients such as vitamin A and vitamin C
Smoked paprika	Rich in vitamins and minerals such as vitamin C and iron, and contains anti-inflammatory properties
Garlic powder	Has been shown to help lower LDL "bad" cholesterol, raise HDL "good" cholesterol, and prevent blood clots. Has anti-cancer properties and contains antioxidants
Onion powder	Contains many cancer fighting properties, supports bone health, and are anti-inflammatory
Oregano	Rich in nutrients and antioxidants, also contains anti-inflammatory properties
Basil	Contains antioxidants, anti-inflammatory, and contains anti-aging properties
Curry powder	Contains anti-cancer properties and helps to reduce risk of heart disease, Alzheimer's, reduce inflammation, and boost bone health
Ground cinnamon	Helps regulate blood sugar, fight bacteria, and contains anti-inflammatory properties
Cayenne pepper	Aides in digestion and supports the metabolism

Equivalent Measure and Weights

Liquid Measures

1 gal=	4 qt=	8 pt=	16 cups=	128 fl oz=	3.79 L
½ gal=	2 qt=	4 pt=	8 cups=	64 fl oz=	1.89 L
¼ gal=	1 qt=	2 pt=	4 cups=	32 fl oz=	.95 L
	½ qt=	1 pt=	2 cups=	16 fl oz=	.47 L
	¼ qt=	½ pt=	1 cup=	8 fl oz=	.24 L

Dry measures

	1 cup=	8 fl oz=	16 tbsp=	48 tsp=	237 ml
	¾ cup=	6 fl oz=	12 tbsp=	36 tsp=	177 ml
	2/3 cup=	5 1/3 fl oz=	10 2/3 tbsp=	32 tsp=	158 ml
	½ cup=	4 fl oz=	8 tbsp=	24 tsp=	118 ml
	1/3 cup=	2 2/3 fl oz=	5 1/3 tbsp=	16 tsp=	79 ml
	¼ cup=	2 fl oz=	4 tbsp=	12 tsp=	59 ml
	1/8 cup=	1 fl oz=	2 tbsp=	6 tsp=	30 ml
			1 tbsp=	3 tsp=	15 ml

This is a user-friendly chart that can be used to easily convert measurements when cooking. You can adjust the number of servings a recipe makes by using this chart.

GF = Gluten Free   DF = Dairy Free   EF = Egg Free

- BLUEBERRY MUESLI (GF, DF, EF)

- LEMON-BERRY RICOTTA PROTEIN PANCAKES (GF)

- HAM & EGG MUFFINS (GF, DF)

- SAUSAGE & RED PEPPER CRUST-LESS QUICHE (GF)

- SAUSAGE STIR-FRY BREAKFAST (GF, DF)

- EGGS & SWEET POTATO HASH (GF)

- SAUSAGE & EGG SCRAMBLE (GF)

BLUEBERRY MUESLI

Yields 6 servings (½ cup servings)

1 cup red quinoa, cooked
13.5 oz. can unsweetened full-fat coconut milk
¼ cup chia seeds
¼ cup ground flaxseed
1 cup organic blueberries
1 tsp. ground cinnamon
stevia extract to taste

In a medium size mixing bowl, add chia seeds, ground flaxseed, stevia, cinnamon, and coconut milk, mixing thoroughly. Fold in cooked quinoa and blueberries. Place in refrigerator for at least 30 minutes to cool.

Nutritional Information: Total Calories 379, Total Fat 26g, Carbohydrates 32g, Sugars 6g, Dietary Fiber 10g, Protein 8g, Sodium 22mg, excellent source of copper

LEMON BERRY RICOTTA PROTEIN PANCAKES

Yields 8 large pancakes

1 ½ cups grass-fed vanilla protein powder
1 cup fresh squeezed lemon juice
1 cup full-fat ricotta cheese
2 organic free-range eggs
2 tbsp. coconut oil, divided
¼ cup filtered water
2 tsp. dried lemon peel
½ tsp. baking soda
2 tsp. baking powder
1 tsp. poppy seeds
¼ tsp. Himalayan sea salt
1 cup frozen blueberries

Blueberry Sauce:
2 cups frozen blueberries
3 tsp. organic coconut sugar
¼ cup filtered water
2 tbsp. fresh squeezed lemon juice
1 ½ tsp. corn starch

Bring blueberries, coconut sugar, and water to a boil in a saucepan. Whisk together the corn starch and lemon juice then add it to the pan and remove from heat.

Mix together protein, baking soda, baking powder, lemon peel, salt, and poppy seeds. In a separate bowl mix together the ricotta, eggs, lemon juice, 1 tbsp. of the coconut oil, and water. Fold the dry ingredients into the wet until well combined. Heat 1 tbsp. of coconut oil in a skillet over medium heat, ladle about ¼ cup of the pancake batter into the skillet and drop in a few frozen blueberries. Once it starts to bubble in the middle, flip and cook on the other side until pancake is cooked through. Repeat process until all pancakes are cooked. Serve immediately with blueberry sauce as topping

Nutritional Information (1 pancake with ¼ cup of blueberry sauce): Total Calories 153, Total Fat 9g, Carbohydrates 12g, Sugars 6g, Dietary Fiber 2g, Protein 8g, Sodium 258mg, good source of vitamin C

HAM & EGG MUFFINS

Yields 12 muffin cups (1 muffin is one serving)

12 slices low-sodium nitrate/nitrite free ham
12 organic free-range eggs
1 cup organic baby spinach leaves
1 ripe avocado, sliced
Himalayan sea salt
Ground black pepper

Preheat the oven to 375 degrees. Place a slice of ham into each muffin hole. Add a few spinach leaves and a slice or two of avocado to each one. Crack an egg into each muffin hole and sprinkle with Himalayan sea salt and black pepper. Bake for 15-20 minutes or until yolks reach desired consistency. Store in a glass container for up to 5 days in the refrigerator. This makes an excellent protein and fat based breakfast!

Nutritional Information: Total Calories 143, Total Fat 8g, Carbohydrates 2g, Sugars 0g, Dietary Fiber 1g, Protein 15g, Sodium 471mg, good source of selenium, choline, vitamin B12, riboflavin, and thiamin

SAUSAGE AND RED PEPPER QUICHE

Yields 8 servings

12 oz. organic mild or hot Italian sausage, antibiotic, hormone, nitrate/nitrite free
6 organic free-range eggs
1 cup red bell pepper, diced
1/3 cup green bell pepper, diced
1/3 cup yellow onion, diced
1 cup mushrooms, diced
1 cup shredded Mexican blend cheese, divided
¼ tsp. ground red pepper
½ tbsp. dried oregano
½ tbsp. dried basil
½ tsp. black pepper
sprinkle of Himalayan sea salt

Preheat the oven to 350 degrees. Brown sausage in a skillet and add mushrooms towards the end. Whisk together eggs, vegetables, spices, and ½ cup of the cheese in a bowl. Coat a 9-inch glass pie dish with olive oil and pour in the egg mixture. Top with the meat and mushroom mixture and sprinkle with sea salt. Bake for 30 minutes or until eggs are set. Add the other ½ cup of cheese on top and return to oven for 2-3 minutes until cheese melts. Slice into 8 pieces and serve immediately.

Nutritional Information: Total Calories 258, Total Fat 19g, Carbohydrates 5g, Sugars 2g, Dietary Fiber 1g, Protein 16g, Sodium 662mg, good source of selenium, vitamin B12, vitamin C, riboflavin, choline, and thiamin

EGGS AND SWEET POTATO HASH

Yields 4 servings

8 organic free-range eggs
2 tbsp. grass-fed butter
2 medium sweet potatoes, peeled and cut into ¼-inch cubes
½ cup white onion (fresh or frozen)
1 medium red onion, chopped
½ cup green pepper (fresh or frozen)
¼ cup jarred sliced jalapeno
2 tsp. minced garlic
2 tbsp. olive oil
1 tsp. ground cumin
½ tsp. garlic powder
¼ tsp. ground chipotle chili powder
Himalayan sea salt and black pepper to taste

In a medium size pot bring water to boil, add sweet potatoes and boil for 6-8 minutes. Drain the water and set aside to dry. In medium size skillet heat 1 tbsp. olive oil on medium-high heat, add onions and peppers, stirring often and cooking until onions become translucent. Remove cooked peppers and onions, set aside on plate. Add remaining olive oil to pan and add sweet potatoes, green peppers, onions, jalapenos, garlic, cumin, chipotle chili powder, salt and pepper, making a single layer. Cook mixture until potatoes are browned, stirring occasionally. Heat butter in skillet on medium heat, cook eggs over easy or sunny-side up. Spoon sweet potato hash on plate and add eggs on top. Serve immediately.

Nutritional Information: Total Calories 210, Total Fat 13g, Carbohydrates 20g, Sugars 6g, Dietary Fiber 3g, Protein 6g, Sodium 191mg, excellent source of vitamin A and choline

SAUSAGE STIR-FRY BREAKFAST

Yields 2 servings

½ lb. organic mild Italian sausage, ground or sliced, nitrate/nitrite free
½ cup onion, diced
4 cups organic spinach or kale

Heat skillet on medium heat. Add diced onions and sauté until soft, then add sausage and cook until browned. Lastly, add greens, reduce heat to medium-low and cover, cook until greens are wilted and soft.
Optional: Top with 1-2 organic free-range eggs over-easy.

Nutritional Information (without eggs): Total Calories 278, Total Fat 19g, Carbohydrates 18g, Sugars 2g, Dietary Fiber 3g, Protein 13g, Sodium 472mg, excellent source of vitamin A, vitamin C, vitamin K, and manganese

SAUSAGE AND EGG SCRAMBLE

Yields 2 servings

6 organic free-range eggs
2 jalapeno dinner sausage links, nitrate/nitrite free
2 cups organic kale or spinach
¼ cup shredded cheese of choice
Himalayan sea salt and pepper to taste
1 tbsp. grass-fed butter for cooking

Heat butter in a skillet over medium-high heat. Add sausages and kale and cook for 2-3 minutes, until sausage is brown. In a separate bowl, whisk eggs and then add to the pan with sausage and kale. Cook until eggs are desired consistency, add cheese and cook for an additional minute. Season with salt and pepper and serve immediately.

Nutritional Information: Total Calories 304, Total Fat 21g, Carbohydrates 6g, Sugars 1g, Dietary Fiber 2g, Protein 24g, Sodium 772mg, excellent source of copper phosphorous, selenium, vitamin A, vitamin B6, vitamin B12, vitamin C, vitamin K, riboflavin, and choline

SALADS & SIDES

- GARLIC & GINGER SAUTEED SWEET PEPPERS (GF, DF, EF)

- SAUTEED GARLIC MUSHROOMS (GF, EF)

- WHITE BEAN SALAD (GF, DF, EF)

- BAKED BEANS (GF, DF, EF)

- CURRIED MUSHROOMS GREEN BEAN & RICE (GF, DF, EF)

- CRIPSY OVEN ROASTED POTATOES (GF, DF, EF)

- CHIPOTLE SWEET POTATO HASH (GF, DF, EF)

- ROASTED SWEET POTATO WITH CARAMELIZED ONIONS (GF, DF, EF)

- ROASTED BUTTERNUT SQUASH WITH GREEN APPLES & WALNUTS (GF, DF, EF)

- SWEET AND SPICY SWEET POTATO FRIES (GF, DF, EF)

- TWICE BAKED CAULIFLOWER MASH (GF, EF)

- CITRUS BROCCOLI KALE SLAW (DF, EF)

- BROCCOLI SLAW SALAD (DF, EF)

- ZUCCHINI & TOMATO SALAD (DF, EF)

- AVOCADO COBB SALAD (GF)

- BLACK & BLEU SALAD (EF)

- CHICKEN SALAD (GF, EF)

- TACO BAKE SALAD (GF, EF)

- QUINOA SHRIMP SALAD (GF, DF, EF)

GARLIC & GINGER SAUTEED SWEET PEPPERS

Yields 2 servings

3 medium size bell peppers (mix orange, red, and yellow), sliced into strips
2 tbsp. coconut oil
1 tbsp. minced garlic
2 tbsp. finely grated fresh ginger (or 1 tsp. ground ginger)
Himalayan sea salt and pepper to taste

Clean and dry the peppers. Cut the top off of each pepper and remove seeds, slice peppers in half and cut into thin strips. In a medium size skillet, heat coconut oil on medium heat. Add pepper strips and cook until soft, stirring frequently. Add garlic, ginger, salt and pepper, tossing until thoroughly coated, cooking for an additional minute or until desired tenderness. Serve immediately.

Nutritional Information: Total Calories 176, Total Fat 14g, Carbohydrates 13g, Sugars 5g, Dietary Fiber 4g, Protein 2g, Sodium 56mg

SAUTEED GARLIC MUSHROOMS

Yields 2 servings

16 oz. baby bella mushrooms, washed and quartered
1 tbsp. olive oil
1 tbsp. grass-fed butter
1 tbsp. minced garlic
1 tsp. garlic powder
1 tsp. dried oregano
1 tsp. dried parsley
Himalayan sea salt and pepper to taste

Gently clean mushrooms with cold water and dry them with a paper towel. Next, trim the stems and slice mushrooms into quarters. In a medium skillet heat olive oil and butter on medium heat, until bubbling. Add the mushrooms, stirring frequently, and cook until browned. Add minced garlic, garlic powder, oregano, and parsley, salt and pepper. Cook for 1 minute, stirring until garlic and herbs are thoroughly mixed. Serve immediately.

Nutritional Information: Total Calories 64, Total Fat 13g, Carbohydrates 14g, Sugars 4g, Dietary Fiber 4g, Protein 6g, Sodium 182mg, excellent source of riboflavin and niacin

WHITE BEAN SALAD

Yields 4 servings

15 oz. can great northern beans, drained and rinsed
1 small lime, juiced (about 1 ½ tbsp.)
2 tbsp. olive oil
½ tbsp. minced garlic
¼ cup green peppers, diced
¼ cup white onions, diced
1 tsp. dried parsley
1 tsp. dried oregano
½ tsp. dried marjoram leaves
¼ tsp. dried lemon peel
Himalayan sea salt and pepper to taste

Rinse and drain beans (once bubbles dissipate while rinsing, you have removed excess sodium). In a small bowl mix together olive oil, lime juice, garlic, parsley, oregano, marjoram leaves, lemon peel, salt and pepper until well blended. Add beans, onion, and peppers, mix thoroughly. Place in refrigerator to marinate for 30 minutes before serving.

Nutritional Information: Total Calories 194, Total Fat 7g, Carbohydrates 25g, Sugars 1g, Dietary Fiber 6g, Protein 8g, Sodium 31mg, good source of vitamin C, folate, and manganese

BAKED BEANS

Yields 8 servings (½ cup servings)

2-15 oz. cans great northern beans, drained and rinsed
3 slices uncured nitrate/nitrite free bacon, cooked and crumbled
1 cup filtered water
¼ cup organic tomato paste
1 medium onion, diced
¼ cup jarred sliced jalapeños
2 tbsp. brown coconut sugar
2 tsp. Dijon mustard (look for gluten free)
1 tsp. garlic powder
Himalayan sea salt and pepper to taste

Combine all ingredients in a saucepan over medium heat and bring to a boil. Reduce heat to a simmer and cook for 8 minutes until sauce thickens. Remove from heat and serve immediately.

Nutritional Information: Total Calories 160, Total Fat 2g, Carbohydrates 28g, Sugars 4g, Dietary Fiber 6g, Protein 10g, Sodium 277mg, good source of phosphorous and folate

CURRIED MUSHROOMS GREEN BEANS & RICE

Yields 4 servings (½ cup servings)

1 tbsp. olive oil
8 oz. baby portabella mushrooms, sliced
1 medium onion, chopped
1 tbsp. minced garlic
1 tsp. curry powder
1 tsp. ground cumin
1 cup unsweetened full-fat coconut milk
1 cup frozen green beans
½ cup basmati rice, dry
4 slices uncured, nitrate/nitrite free bacon, cooked
Himalayan sea salt and pepper to taste

Heat olive oil in medium size skillet on medium-high heat; add mushrooms, onion, and garlic. Stir occasionally and cook until onions are translucent. Add curry, cumin, and coconut milk, bring to a boil. Stir in green beans and rice, cover and reduce heat to low. Simmer mixture until rice is tender and moisture is absorbed. Crumble and add bacon to rice mixture and season with salt and pepper to taste.

Nutritional Information: Total Calories 313, Total Fat 20g, Carbohydrates 29g, Sugars 4g, Dietary Fiber 4g, Protein 7g, Sodium 150mg, good source of copper, selenium, and niacin

CRISPY OVEN ROASTED POTATOES

Yields 6 servings (½ cup servings)

24 oz. baby yellow potatoes, quartered
2 tbsp. olive oil
1 tsp. garlic powder
½ tsp. red pepper flakes
1 tsp. dried oregano
½ tsp. chipotle chili powder
Himalayan sea salt and pepper to taste

Preheat oven to 375 degrees. Combine all ingredients in a bowl and mix well to coat potatoes. Spread evenly on baking sheet and bake for 45 minutes or until crispy.

Nutritional Information: Total Calories 100, Total Fat 5g, Carbohydrates 13g, Sugars 1g, Dietary Fiber 2g, Protein 2g, Sodium 102mg

CHIPOTLE SWEET POTATO HASH

Yields 4 servings (½ cup servings)

2 medium sweet potatoes, peeled and cut into ¼-inch cubes
½ cup white onion, diced (fresh or frozen)
1 medium red onion, chopped
½ cup green pepper, diced (fresh or frozen)
¼ cup jarred sliced jalapenos
2 tsp. minced garlic
2 tbsp. olive oil
1 tsp. ground cumin
½ tsp. garlic powder
¼ tsp. chipotle chili powder
Himalayan sea salt and black pepper to taste

In a medium size pot, bring water to boil, add sweet potatoes and boil for 6-8 minutes or until soft. Drain the water and set aside to dry. In medium size skillet heat 1 tbsp. of olive oil on medium-high heat, add onions and peppers, stirring often and cooking until onions become translucent. Remove cooked peppers and onions, set aside on plate. Add remaining olive oil to pan and add sweet potatoes, green peppers, onions, jalapenos, garlic, cumin, chipotle chili powder, salt and pepper, making a single layer. Cook mixture until potatoes are browned stirring occasionally. Serve immediately.

Nutritional Information: Total Calories 144, Total Fat 7g, Carbohydrates 19g, Sugars 6g, Dietary Fiber 3g, Protein 2g, Sodium 135mg, good source of manganese, vitamin A, and vitamin C

ROASTED SWEET POTATOES WITH CARAMELIZED ONIONS

Yields 6, ½ cup servings

3 medium sweet potatoes, cubed
1 red onion, sliced thin
2 tbsp. olive oil
1 tsp. chipotle chili powder
1 tsp. paprika
1 tsp. onion powder
1 tsp. garlic powder
Himalayan sea salt and pepper to taste

Preheat oven to 375 degrees. Combine all ingredients in a bowl and mix well to coat potatoes. Spread evenly on baking sheet and bake for 45 minutes or until crispy.

Nutritional Information: Total Calories 144, Total Fat 5g, Carbohydrates 24g, Sugars 5g, Fiber 4g, Protein 2g, Sodium 128 mg, excellent source of vitamin A

ROASTED BUTTERNUT SQUASH WITH GREEN APPLES & WALNUTS

Yields 4 servings

12 oz. frozen and chopped butternut squash
2 medium organic green apples, chopped into ½-inch cubes
1 tbsp. molasses
Himalayan sea salt to taste
2 tbsp. olive oil
½ cup chopped walnuts
½ tsp ground cinnamon

Nutritional Information: Total Calories 240, Total Fat 17g, Carbohydrates 24g, Sugars 12g, Dietary Fiber 4g, Protein 3g, Sodium 6mg

SWEET & SPICY SWEET POTATO FRIES

Yields 4-6 servings (1 cup servings)

4 small sweet potatoes, sliced into halves and then cut into ¼-inch strips
1 tbsp. olive oil
2 tsp. garlic powder
1 tsp. smoked paprika
½ tsp. Himalayan sea salt
1 tbsp. brown sugar
¼ tsp. ground red pepper

Preheat oven to 400 degrees. Place sweet potato strips into large mixing bowl and drizzle with olive oil, mix and coat and then add all spices and mix again. Bake for 20-25 minutes.

Nutritional Information: Total Calories 107, Total Fat 3g, Carbohydrates 19g, Sugars 5g, Dietary Fiber 3g, Protein 2g, Sodium 256mg

TWICE BAKED CAULIFLOWER MASH

Yields 4-6 servings (½ cup servings)

1 large head of cauliflower
2 tbsp. grass-fed butter
2 oz. full-fat cream cheese, softened
1 tsp. garlic powder
½ tsp. Himalayan sea salt
¼ tsp. ground black pepper
1/3 cup Monterey Jack shredded cheese
chopped green onions for garnish

Preheat oven to 400 degrees. Clean and cut cauliflower into small pieces. Bring a large pot of water to a boil over high heat. Add cauliflower pieces to the pot and boil for 6-8 minute or until soft. Drain well and pat with paper towels to remove excess water. Transfer cauliflower into a food processor or blender, add butter, cream cheese, garlic powder, sea salt, and pepper. Blend until mixture is smooth and creamy. Transfer mixture into a baking dish, sprinkle with cheese and bake until cheese is melted. Top with chopped green onions if desired for garnish.

Nutritional Information: Total Calories 155, Total Fat 11g, Carbohydrates 12g, Sugars 5g, Dietary Fiber 5g, Protein 6g, Sodium 410mg, good source of vitamin B6, vitamin C, vitamin k, and folate

CITRUS BROCCOLI KALE SLAW

Yields 4 servings

2 cups finely chopped kale, stems removed
2 cups shredded broccoli or pre-packaged broccoli slaw
6-8 fresh mint leaves, finely chopped, stems removed
¼ cup sunflower seeds
¼ cup low-sugar dried cranberries

Citrus Dressing:
2 tbsp. fresh squeezed orange juice
1 tsp. Dijon mustard (look for gluten free)
2 tbsp. apple cider vinegar
2 tbsp. raw honey
2 tbsp. olive oil
¼ tsp. ground ginger

Whisk together all dressing ingredients and refrigerate for 30 minutes. Combine kale, broccoli slaw, mint, sunflower seeds, and cranberries in a large salad bowl. Toss with dressing and serve immediately.

Nutritional Information: Total Calories 197, Total Fat 11g, Carbohydrates 23g, Sugars 15g, Dietary Fiber 3g, Protein 4g, Sodium 76mg, excellent source of vitamin C and vitamin K

BROCCOLI SLAW SALAD

Yields 6-8 servings

2 10 oz. pre-packaged broccoli slaw bags
¼ cup olive oil
¼ cup white wine vinegar
¼ cup apple cider vinegar
½ tsp. garlic powder
Himalayan salt and pepper to taste

Mix olive oil, vinegars, garlic powder, salt and pepper in a small bowl, set aside. In a large bowl combine pre-packaged broccoli slaw and dressing mixture, mix until broccoli slaw is well coated. Refrigerate for 30 minutes and serve.

Nutritional Information: Total Calories 89, Total Fat 8g, Carbohydrates 4g, Sugars 1g, Dietary Fiber 1g, Protein 1g, Sodium 40mg, good source of vitamin C and vitamin K

ZUCCHINI TOMATO SALAD

Yields 4 servings (1 cup servings)

3 small zucchini, sliced with a mandoline or very thinly with a knife
1 pint grape tomatoes
1/3 cup olive oil
1/3 cup apple cider vinegar
1 tbsp. dried oregano
1 tbsp. dried basil
¼ tsp. Himalayan sea salt

Combine all ingredients in a bowl and mix well. Marinate covered in the refrigerator for at least an hour before serving.

Nutritional Information: Total Calories 199, Total Fat 19g, Carbohydrates 7g, Sugars 5g, Dietary Fiber 3g, Protein 2g, Sodium 159mg, good source of vitamin C, vitamin E, and vitamin K

AVOCADO COBB SALAD

Yields 2 servings

2 cups organic baby spinach
2 cups red-leaf lettuce, shredded
2 slices uncured bacon, nitrate/nitrite free, cooked until crispy
2 hard-boiled organic free-range eggs
½ cup cherry tomatoes
1 oz. crumbled blue cheese

Avocado Sauce (use as dressing):
1 large avocado
½ cup plain Greek yogurt (10% milk-fat is best, use 2% at lowest)
1 medium lime, juiced
½ tsp. garlic powder
Himalayan sea salt and pepper to taste

Combine avocado, yogurt, lime juice, garlic powder, salt and pepper into food processor or blender, blend until smooth. Transfer to small bowl and refrigerate for 30 minutes.

Place spinach and red-leaf lettuce on a plate. Layer with tomato, egg, blue cheese, avocado slices, and crumbled bacon. Drizzle avocado sauce on as desired for the dressing and serve immediately. Recipe can easily be doubled or tripled to serve more. Add grilled chicken for an extra protein kick!

Nutritional Information (salad with 2 tbsp. of avocado dressing): Total Calories 363, Total Fat 28g, Carbohydrates 15g, Sugars 3g, Dietary Fiber 9g, Protein 17g, Sodium 496mg, excellent source of vitamin A and vitamin K

BLACK & BLEU SALAD

Yields 2 servings

½ lb. organic grass-fed sirloin steak
2 cups romaine lettuce, washed and chopped
2 cups green-leaf lettuce, washed and chopped
½ cup organic blueberries
½ cup organic strawberries, sliced
¼ cup chopped pecans
½ an avocado, sliced
2 oz. crumbled blue cheese
balsamic vinegar and olive oil for dressing

Place lettuce on plates. Layer cheese and pecans in the middle of the lettuce. Add berries and drizzle with balsamic vinegar and olive oil. Warm steak if desired and place on top of salad. Serve immediately.

Nutritional Information: Total Calories 617, Total Fat 23g, Carbohydrates 20g, Sugars 10g, Dietary Fiber 10g, Protein 33g, Sodium 476mg, excellent source of copper, phosphorus, zinc, vitamin B6, vitamin B12, vitamin K, folate, and niacin

Yields 4 servings (1 cup servings)

2 cups cooked and shredded organic chicken breast, hormone and antibiotic free
1 cup red grapes, quartered
¼ chopped pecans
½ cup celery, chopped
1 cup Greek yogurt (10% milk-fat is best, use 2% at minimum)
Optional: stevia for added sweetness
Himalayan sea salt and pepper to taste

To cook chicken, place chicken breast on foil piece about 1-foot long and season with sea salt, pepper, and garlic powder to taste. Wrap up tight and bake at 375 degrees for 40 minutes. Once chicken is cool, shred and set aside 2 cups. Mix all ingredients together and refrigerate for at least 30 minutes before serving. Serve as a lettuce wrap, with celery slices, on a sandwich thin, or with a tortilla.

Nutritional Information: Total Calories 251, Total Fat 11g, Carbohydrates 14g, Sugars 7g, Dietary Fiber 1g, Protein 23g, Sodium 150mg, good source of niacin and vitamin B6

TACO BAKE SALAD

*** this is a casserole dish that you make into a salad, however it works great
just as a one dish wonder (it's my mom's favorite!!)**

Yields 6 servings

1 lb. organic grass-fed 85% ground beef, cooked and drained
1 cup brown rice, dry
2 cups filtered water
15 oz. can black beans, rinsed
10 oz. can organic, no salt added diced tomatoes
4 oz. can diced jalapeño peppers
1 cup green peppers, diced (fresh or frozen)
1 cup onions, diced (fresh or frozen)
1 cup Monterey jack cheese, shredded
2 avocados, sliced
12 cups organic spinach leaves or lettuce

Taco Seasoning Mix:
2 tbsp. chili powder
1 tbsp. ground cumin
½ tbsp. dried oregano leaves
2 tsp. garlic powder
2 tsp. onion powder
½ tsp. crushed red pepper flakes
½ tsp. Himalayan sea salt
½ tsp. ground black pepper

Mix seasonings together in small bowl until well blended.

Preheat oven to 350 degrees. Cook ground beef in a medium size skillet on medium
heat, rinse, drain, and set aside. In a 9x13 glass baking dish add rice and water.
Add ground beef on top of rice and water, and cover beef with taco seasoning.
Layer black beans, tomatoes, jalapenos, green peppers, and onions on top of beef.
Cover with foil and bake for 45 minutes to 1 hour, until rice is cooked. Cover with 1
cup of shredded Monterey jack cheese, and cook until melted. Serve immediately
with 1/3 of and avocado sliced and 2 cups of lettuce or spinach leaves.

Nutritional Information: Total Calories 434, Total Fat 16g, Carbohydrates 45g,
Sugars 4g, Dietary Fiber 10g, Protein 28g, Sodium 304mg, excellent source of
copper, phosphorous, zinc, vitamin B6, vitamin B12, vitamin C and vitamin K

QUINOA SHRIMP SALAD

Yields 2 servings

1/3 cup red quinoa, dry
2/3 cup filtered water
10-12 jumbo shrimp, cooked
1 cup organic cherry tomatoes, halved
½ cucumber, diced
¼ cup red onion, diced
2 tbsp. fresh lime juice
½ tsp. ground cumin
Himalayan sea salt and pepper to taste
2 cups organic baby spinach

Combine quinoa and water in a saucepan and bring to a boil. Once boiling, reduce heat to low, cover and cook for 20-25 minutes until water is evaporated and quinoa is fluffy and light. Transfer to a small bowl and refrigerate for at least 30 minutes. Combine tomatoes, red onion, cucumber, lime juice, cumin, sea salt, and pepper in a bowl. Once quinoa is chilled, add it to the vegetable mixture and stir to combine. Scoop 1 cup of the quinoa mixture on top of 1 cup of spinach, squeeze lime juice over salad and serve.

Nutritional Information: Total Calories 164, Total Fat 2g, Carbohydrates 25g, Sugars 3g, Dietary Fiber 4g, Protein 12g, Sodium 141mg, excellent source of vitamin A, vitamin K, and manganese

MAIN DISHES

- BUTTERNUT SQUASH PEAR SOUP (GF, DF, EF)

- MEDITERRANEAN BURGER (GF)

- BACON CHEDDAR JALAPENO BURGER (GF)

- GORGONZOLA BURGER (GF)

- SLOPPY JOE STUFFED PEPPERS (EF)

- CHILI (GF, DF, EF)

- SAUSAGE SQUASH LASAGNA (GF, EF)

- SPAGHETTI SQUASH AND MEATBALLS (GF, DF, EF)

- BACON WRAPPED STEAK KABOBS (GF, DF, EF)

- BEEF AND BROCCOLI STIR FRY (DF, EF)

- MEXICAN STEAK BOWL (GF, DF, EF)

- MINI MEAT LOAVES

- STEAK & VEGETABLE STIR FRY (GF, DF, EF)

- BEEF & MUSHROOM RAGOUT (DF, EF)

- BEEF CURRY (GF, DF, EF)

- ZUCCHINI TACO BOATS (GF, EF)

- SPICY STEAK LETTUCE WRAPS (GF, DF, EF)

- SPAGHETTI SQUASH LASAGNA (GF)

- CHICKEN TERIYAKI LETTUCE WRAPS (EF)

- THAI PEANUT CHICKEN LETTUCE WRAPS (DF, EF)

- CHICKEN STUFFED PORTABELLAS (GF, EF)

- ITALIAN CHICKEN VEGETABLE SOUP (GF, EF)

- BACON WRAPPED CHICKEN TENDERS (GF, DF, EF)

- CHICKEN CURRY (GF, DF, EF)

- ZUCHINNI CHICKEN ALFREDO (GF, EF)

- WHITE CHICKEN CHILI (DF, EF)

- SAGE CHICKEN AND FALL VEGETABLES (DF, EF)

- CHICKEN FAJITA BAKE (GF, EF)

- CHICKEN SPINACH ARTICHOKE BAKE (GF, DF, EF)

- LEMON DILL SALMON (GF, EF)

- PAN SEARED SALMON W/ VEGETABLES (GF, DF, EF)

- LEMON PEPPER COD (GF, DF, EF)

- SHRIMP TACOS (EF)

- SPAGHETTI SQUASH SHRIMP SCAMPI (GF, EF)

- SHRIMP CURRY (GF, DF, EF)

- SHRIMP STUFFED PORTABELLAS (GF, EF)

- SWEET & SPICY RUBBED TENDERLOIN (DF, EF)

- MEDITERRANEAN STUFFED TENDERLOIN (EF)

- SWEET POTATO SAUSAGE SKILLET (GF, DF, EF)

- STUFFED MUSHROOMS W/ BLUEBERRY GLAZE (EF)

BUTTERNUT SQUASH PEAR SOUP

Yields 4 servings (2 cups is one serving)

2 12 oz. bags frozen butternut squash, cubed
4 organic pears, peeled and cubed
3 tbsp. olive oil
1 medium onion, diced or 1 cup frozen diced onions
1 tbsp. minced garlic
¼ tsp. dried thyme
2 cups organic vegetable stock (look for gluten free)
Himalayan sea salt and pepper to taste
½ cup unsweetened full-fat coconut milk

Add pears, butternut squash, and olive oil to food processor and blend until smooth. Heat 1 tbsp. of olive oil in large stock pot on medium heat. Add onion, garlic and thyme, cooking until translucent. Add butternut squash pear mixture, vegetable stock and salt and pepper to stock pot, cooking on low heat for about 15 minutes. Stir in coconut milk and cook an additional 5 minutes. Serve immediately and enjoy.

Nutritional Information: Total Calories 225, Total Fat 12g, Carbohydrates 32g, Sugars 15g, Dietary Fiber 6g, Protein 2g, Sodium 59mg, excellent source of copper, vitamin B6, thiamin, and riboflavin

MEDITERRANEAN BURGER

Yields 8 burgers

2 lb. organic grass-fed 85% ground beef
8 oz. container baby bella mushrooms, finely diced
12 oz. roasted red peppers, finely diced (look for gluten free)
2 cups organic baby spinach, finely chopped
2 organic, free-range eggs
1 tsp. dried oregano
1 tsp. dried basil
1 tsp. garlic powder
¼ tsp. Himalayan sea salt
4 oz. crumbled full-fat feta cheese
8 large green-leaf lettuce leaves
2 avocados, sliced
additional roasted red peppers for topping

Dice mushrooms, peppers, and spinach very fine. Add feta cheese and mix well. In a separate, large bowl, combine beef, egg, and seasonings, mixing thoroughly. Fold in vegetable mixture until evenly distributed. Form patties and cook in skillet on medium-high heat for 2-3 minutes on each side or until desired temperature. Place patty on a piece of green-leaf lettuce, top with red peppers and avocado and enjoy!

Nutritional Information: Total Calories 177, Total Fat 11g, Carbohydrates 2g, Sugars 1g, Dietary Fiber 1g, Protein 17g, Sodium 170mg, excellent source of zinc, vitamin B12, and vitamin K

BACON AND CHEDDAR JALAPENO BURGER

Yields 6 burgers

1 lb. organic grass-fed 85% ground beef
1 organic free-range egg
½ lb. uncured nitrate/nitrite free bacon
1 small onion, diced
¼ cup jalapenos, diced (jarred or fresh)
1 tsp. garlic powder
½ tsp. red pepper flakes
1 tsp. dried oregano
Himalayan sea salt and pepper to taste
4 oz. extra sharp cheddar cheese, cubed (slice block in half lengthwise and then into ¼-inch cubes)
12 portabella mushroom caps

Cook bacon in a skillet over medium-high heat until crispy. Remove from heat and place on paper towel. Chop bacon into small pieces. Combine beef, onion, bacon, jalapeños, egg, garlic powder, red pepper flakes, oregano, sea salt and pepper until well mixed. Fold in cheese cubes last. Form into ½ cup balls then smash down to form patties and cook in skillet on medium-high heat. Place mushroom caps gill side down on a rimmed baking sheet. Brush tops of the caps with olive oil and sprinkle with sea salt, pepper, and garlic powder. Broil mushrooms for about 5 minutes and remove from oven. Place burger between two of the mushroom caps and serve immediately.

Nutritional Information: Total Calories 461, Total Fat 34g, Carbohydrates 11g, Sugars 4g, Dietary Fiber 3g, Protein 30g, Sodium 525mg, good source of copper, selenium, phosphorus, and niacin

GORGONZOLA BURGER

Yields 5 burgers

1 lb. organic grass-fed 85% ground beef
1 organic free-range egg
1 cup organic kale, shredded (may substitute spinach if desired)
½ pint button mushrooms, diced
¼ cup gorgonzola cheese
¼ tsp. cayenne pepper (optional for extra kick)
¼ tsp. crushed red pepper flakes
½ tbsp. ground cumin
½ tsp. dried oregano
1 tsp. garlic powder
1 tsp. onion powder
¼ tsp. Himalayan sea salt
1 beefsteak tomato, sliced
1 avocado, sliced
1 head green-leaf lettuce

Combine beef, egg, mushrooms, kale, cheese, and seasonings. Form patties to desired size and sauté in a pan until cooked thoroughly. Place burger inside lettuce leaf and top with avocado and tomato. Wrap it up and enjoy!

Nutritional Information: Total Calories 237, Total Fat 14g, Carbohydrates 6g, Sugars 2g, Dietary Fiber 1g, Protein 21g, Sodium 144mg, excellent source of zinc, vitamin B12, and vitamin K

SLOPPY JOE STUFFED PEPPERS

Yields 4 servings

1 lb. organic grass-fed 85% ground beef
4 medium yellow peppers
1 medium onion, chopped
1 10.5 oz. can low sodium tomato soup
½ cup low sugar ketchup
1 tsp. Worcestershire sauce
1 ½ tbsp. white vinegar
2 tbsp. brown sugar
1 tbsp. chili powder
½ cup shredded Monterey jack cheese
sliced green onions and parsley for garnish

Preheat oven to 350 degrees. In a medium skillet, cook ground beef and onions on medium heat, and drain excess grease. Add tomato soup, ketchup, Worcestershire sauce, vinegar, brown sugar, and chili powder. Let simmer for 20 minutes on low heat. Cut top off peppers and remove seeds. Fill peppers with sloppy Joe mixture, place in glass baking dish (I used 8 x 10) and bake in oven for 10-15 minutes. Remove from oven, sprinkle cheese on each pepper and bake until cheese is melted. Garnish with sliced green onions and parsley.

Nutritional Information: Total Calories 339, Total Fat 17g, Carbohydrates 21g, Sugars 9g, Dietary Fiber 2g, Protein 27g, Sodium 206mg, excellent source of zinc, vitamin B12, and vitamin C

CHILI

Yields 8 servings

1 lb. organic grass-fed 85% ground beef
1 15oz. can dark red kidney beans, drained and rinsed
1 15 oz. can red kidney beans, drained and rinsed
1 tbsp. minced garlic
1 medium yellow onion, diced
4 large tomatoes
1 10 oz. can diced tomatoes and green chilies
¼ cup sliced jalapenos (jarred or fresh)
6 oz. can organic tomato sauce
1 tbsp. chili powder
1 tbsp. ground cumin
1 tbsp. garlic powder
1 tsp. onion powder
1 tsp. cocoa powder
1 tbsp. dried oregano
1 cup filtered water

Brown beef, garlic, and onion in a skillet until onions are translucent and beef is cooked through. Drain and rinse with water. Add beef mixture to a crockpot and add all other ingredients. Cook on low for 6-8 hours, cut tomatoes open and slice into bite-size pieces, mix well and serve immediately.

Nutritional Information: Total Calories 243, Total Fat 7g, Carbohydrates 27g, Sugars 8g, Dietary Fiber 9g, Protein 18g, Sodium 252mg, good source of zinc and vitamin B12

SAUSAGE SPAGHETTI SQUASH LASAGNA

Yields 6-8 servings

2 lb. spaghetti squash
12 oz. bag frozen, cubed butternut squash, thawed
1 lb. Italian sausage, hormone and antibiotic free
1 ½ cups 4% milk-fat cottage cheese, small curd
15 oz. can organic, no salt added diced tomatoes, drained
6 oz. can organic tomato paste
½ cup filtered water
1 ½ cups mozzarella cheese, shredded
1 small sweet onion, thinly sliced
1 tbsp. minced garlic
1 tsp. dried basil
1 tsp. dried oregano
Himalayan sea salt and pepper to taste

To roast spaghetti squash, preheat oven to 350 degrees. Slice spaghetti squash in half, remove seeds and place face down on a baking sheet. Bake in the oven for 25 minutes, remove from oven, and set aside until cool to touch. Using a fork, scrape squash out of shells and distribute evenly in the bottom of a 9 x 13 baking dish. Set aside.

In food processor, blend butternut squash, tomatoes, tomato paste, oregano, basil, salt and pepper until well blended and set aside. In medium size skillet, cook Italian sausage on medium heat, add onions and minced garlic until tender. Add butternut squash sauce and ½ cup water, cooking until sauce reduces and is slightly thicker, approximately 5 minutes. Add an even layer of cottage cheese on top of the spaghetti squash and top with meat sauce. Bake in the oven uncovered for 30 minutes at 350 degrees. Top with mozzarella cheese and place back in the oven until cheese is melted. Let cool for 10 minutes and then serve with a mixed greens salad to complete the meal.

Nutritional Information: Total Calories 400, Total Fat 25g, Carbohydrates 27g, Sugars 9g, Dietary Fiber 2g, Protein 21g, Sodium 764mg, excellent source of vitamin A, vitamin B12, and thiamin

SPAGHETTI SQUASH AND MEATBALLS

Yields 6 servings

6 lb. spaghetti squash
2 lb. organic grass-fed 85% ground beef
1 large yellow onion, diced
8 oz. baby bella mushrooms, diced
1 cup organic baby spinach, minced
1 tbsp. dried oregano
1 tbsp. dried basil
1 tsp. garlic powder
1 tsp. onion powder

Preheat oven to 350 degrees. Cut squash in half and remove seeds with a spoon. Place cut side down on a baking sheet and add ½ cup of water to the baking sheet. Bake for 30 minutes or until tender, remove from oven and set aside until cool to touch. Once cool, run a fork along the inside of the squash and it will pull apart into "noodles". Transfer to a bowl and set aside.

Combine mushrooms, onions, and spinach with garlic powder, onion powder, oregano, and basil. Add beef and mix very well to combine evenly. Scoop out ½ cup servings of the beef mixture, form into balls and place into muffin tins. Bake for 30 minutes or until 165 degrees.

Tomato Sauce:
*** you may also use jarred pasta sauce that is low sugar/low sodium. Try to find one with <5g sugar per serving*

14.5 oz. can organic, no salt added diced tomatoes
6 oz. can organic tomato paste
8 oz. organic tomato sauce
1 tbsp. dried basil
1 tbsp. dried oregano
1 tsp. garlic powder
1 tsp. onion powder
Himalayan sea salt and pepper to taste

In a small saucepan over medium-high heat, combine all ingredients and stir well to combine. Once sauce reaches a boil, reduce heat and simmer for 10 minutes. Divide spaghetti squash evenly, top with 2 meatballs, and ½ cup of tomato sauce. Serve immediately.

Nutritional Information: Total Calories 398, Total Fat 17g, Carbohydrates 30g, Sugars 14g, Dietary Fiber 7g, Protein 33g, Sodium 318mg, excellent source of selenium, zinc, vitamin B6, vitamin B12, and niacin

BACON WRAPPED SIRLOIN KABOBS

Yields 6-8 kabobs (1 kabob is one serving)

1-1.5 lb. organic grass-fed sirloin steak
1 lb. baby golden Yukon potatoes, steamed
1 lb. uncured, nitrate/nitrite free bacon
3 bell peppers of different colors, sliced into ½-inch pieces
1 yellow onion, sliced into ½-inch pieces
8 oz. mushrooms
¼ cup rice vinegar
¼ cup olive oil
¼ cup Sriracha sauce
¼ tsp. cayenne pepper
¼ tsp. crushed red pepper flakes
½ tbsp. ground cumin
½ tsp. dried oregano
1 tsp. garlic powder
1 tsp. onion powder
¼ tsp. Himalayan sea salt
kabob sticks

Slice the sirloin into 1-inch cubes. Whisk together olive oil, Sriracha, rice vinegar, and a dash of sea salt. Pour over sirloin and let marinate for at least 30 minutes. Chop the peppers and onion into 1 inch pieces. Place one of the steamed potatoes at the end of the kabob, then wrap a piece of sirloin in bacon and add to the stick. Add peppers, onion, and mushroom, then more sirloin and repeat as desired. Add another potato at the other end of the kabob. Repeat this process until all ingredients are used. Mix all spices together and then sprinkle each kabob with seasoning to taste. Grill for 4-5 minutes on each side or until meat reaches desired temperature.

Nutritional Information: Total Calories 233, Total Fat 10g, Carbohydrates 20g, Sugars 3g, Dietary Fiber 3g, Protein 16g, Sodium 85mg, excellent source of zinc, vitamin B12, and vitamin K

BEEF AND BROCCOLI STIR-FRY

Yields 4 servings

Steak Marinade:

1 lb. grass-fed organic London beef broil, sliced into ¼-inch strips

1 small lime, juiced (1 ½ tbsp.)

3 tbsp. low sodium soy sauce

½ tsp. ground ginger

Vegetable Stir-Fry:

1 tbsp. olive oil

1 tbsp. minced garlic

8 mini sweet bell peppers (red, yellow, orange) sliced into ¼-inch rings

½ lb. broccoli crowns

Sauce:

¼ cup low sodium soy sauce

2 tsp. corn starch

½ tsp. ground ginger

½ tsp. garlic powder

Himalayan sea salt and pepper to taste

1 tsp. sesame seeds

Rice:

1 cup basmati rice, dry

2 ½ cups filtered water

1 tbsp. olive oil

In a small bowl, combine lime juice, soy sauce, ginger, and steak slices, place in refrigerator for 10 minutes. In another small bowl, combine soy sauce, corn starch, ground ginger, garlic powder, salt and pepper, set aside. In a small saucepan combine rice, water, and oil. Bring to boil and reduce heat to low, cover and cook for 20 minutes or until water is absorbed, fluff rice with a fork and cover until ready to serve. Heat olive oil in a medium skillet on medium heat, add garlic and broccoli, cook for 2 minutes and add pepper rings. Reduce heat and cook vegetables until tender, approximately 2-3 minutes. Remove vegetables from skillet and set aside. In the same skillet, add steak with marinade and cook on medium heat until steak is no longer pink, approximately 3 minutes. Add sauce to skillet, stirring frequently until well blended. Add vegetables, toss thoroughly, then add sesame seeds and remove from heat. Serve immediately with rice. Enjoy this recipe it is absolutely delicious!

Nutritional Information: Total Calories 463, Total Fat 12g, Carbohydrates 54g, Sugars 4g, Dietary Fiber 3g, Protein 36g, Sodium 1314mg

MEXICAN STEAK BOWL

Yields 4 servings

1 ½ lb. organic grass-fed sirloin steak, thinly sliced

15 oz. can black beans, drained and rinsed well

10 oz. can diced tomatoes with green chilies, drained and rinsed

16 oz. mushrooms, sliced

2 medium yellow onions, sliced

1 tsp. garlic powder

1 tsp. ground cumin

1 tsp. onion powder

1 tsp. chili powder

¼ tsp. Himalayan sea salt

¼ tsp. black pepper

8 cups green-leaf lettuce, shredded

1 tbsp. olive oil

Optional toppings: guacamole, mango salsa (recipes can be found in snacks/dips section)

Heat olive oil in skillet over medium-high heat. Sauté onions and mushrooms until onions are translucent. Add sliced steak and cook for about 3 minutes. Add in black beans, tomatoes and chilies, and all seasonings. Toss until well mixed, add more salt and pepper to taste. Place green-leaf lettuce onto plate, top with steak and vegetable mixture and then add guacamole and mango salsa on top if desired. Serve immediately.

Nutritional Information: Total Calories 393, Total Fat 10g, Carbohydrates 32g, Sugars 7g, Dietary Fiber 12g, Protein 44g, Sodium 277mg, excellent source of copper, phosphorous, selenium, zinc, vitamin B6, vitamin B12, vitamin K, and niacin

MINI MEAT LOAVES

Yields 4 servings (2 meatloaves is one serving)

1 lb. organic grass-fed 85% ground beef
1/3 cup onion, chopped (fresh or frozen)
1/3 cup green bell pepper, chopped (fresh or frozen)
¼ cup grated parmesan cheese
½ tsp. Italian seasoning
¼ tsp. ground black pepper
¼ tsp. cayenne pepper
¼ tsp. chili powder
½ tsp. garlic powder
¾ tsp. kosher salt
1 organic free-range egg

Sauce:
¼ cup low-sugar ketchup
1 tbsp. Sriracha sauce
½ tsp. ground cumin
1 tsp. Worcestershire sauce

Preheat oven to 350 degrees. In medium bowl, combine beef, onion, green bell pepper, Parmesan cheese, Italian seasoning, black pepper, cayenne pepper, chili powder, garlic powder, salt and egg, mixing thoroughly until all ingredients are evenly blended. In separate small bowl, mix ketchup, Sriracha sauce, cumin, and Worcestershire Sauce until well blended, set aside. Divide beef mixture into approximately ½ cup servings and pack into silicone muffin holders or a regular muffin tin. Pack mixture down pressing a slight indention into the center of each mini meatloaf. Bake for 20 minutes, remove from the oven, add ½ tbsp. of sauce to the top of each mini meatloaf and spread to the sides. Bake an additional 10 minutes, remove from oven and serve.

Nutritional Information: Total Calories 252, Total Fat 14g, Carbohydrates 7g, Sugars 5g, Dietary Fiber 1g, Protein 23g, Sodium 874mg, excellent source of zinc and vitamin B12

Yields 6 servings

Steak:
2 lb. organic grass-fed sirloin, cut into strips
1 tbsp. olive oil
6 tbsp. liquid aminos (alternative to soy sauce)
1 tsp. onion powder
1 tsp. garlic powder
3 tbsp. hot sauce (look for gluten free)

Vegetable Mixture:
2 yellow onions, sliced
1 red onion, sliced
1 lb. mini bell peppers, sliced
1 tbsp. olive oil
1 small crown fresh broccoli, cut into florets
1 tbsp. minced garlic
½ tsp. garlic powder
½ tsp. onion powder
Himalayan sea salt and black pepper to taste

Whisk together olive oil, liquid aminos, onion powder, garlic powder, and hot sauce for the steak mixture and set aside. Heat olive oil in skillet over medium heat, add minced garlic and brown for 2 minutes. Add all vegetables, garlic powder, onion powder, sea salt and pepper, cooking until vegetables are al dente. Remove vegetables from skillet, heat the other tbsp. of olive oil and add the steak, cooking for 2 minutes. Add the sauce and cook for an additional 2-3 minutes or until steak is cooked through. Serve steak with vegetables over rice.

Nutritional Information: Total Calories 279, Total Fat 10g, Carbohydrates 17g, Sugars 5g, Dietary Fiber 3g, Protein 32g, Sodium 340mg, excellent source of selenium, zinc, vitamin B6, vitamin B12, vitamin C, vitamin k, and niacin

BEEF AND MUSHROOM RAGOUT

Yields 4 servings

2 lb. grass-fed London broil
8 oz. baby bella mushrooms
8 oz. bag baby carrots
1 large red potato, cubed
1 large yellow onion, sliced
6 oz. can organic tomato paste
1 cup organic vegetable broth
¼ cup Worcestershire sauce
2 tbsp. minced garlic
1 tsp. garlic powder
1 tsp. onion powder
1 tsp. rosemary
3 bay leaves

Combine all ingredients in a crockpot and place beef whole on top. Cook on low for 8 hours.

Nutritional Information: Total Calories 392, Total Fat 7g, Carbohydrates 37g, Sugars 13g, Dietary Fiber 6g, Protein 46g, Sodium 496mg, excellent source of copper, phosphorous, selenium, zinc, vitamin B6, vitamin B12, riboflavin, and niacin

BEEF CURRY

Yields 7 servings

2 ½ lb. organic grass-fed beef shoulder roast, cubed
2 medium sweet potatoes, peeled and diced into ½-inch pieces
3 large carrots, peeled and sliced into ¼-inch rounds
2 parsnips, peeled and sliced into ¼-inch rounds
1 ½ tbsp. minced garlic
2 tsp. ground ginger
14.5 oz. can organic, no salt added diced tomatoes
13.5 oz. can unsweetened full-fat coconut milk
2 tbsp. curry powder
½ tsp. Himalayan sea salt
1 tbsp. corn starch

Mix all ingredients in crock pot except the corn starch and cook on low for 6-8 hours. Remove meat and vegetables and set aside. Whisk corn starch into the remaining juice in the crock pot until it thickens. Plate meat and vegetables over rice and top with curry sauce.

Nutritional Information: Total Calories 697, Total Fat 43g, Carbohydrates 45g, Sugars 8g, Dietary Fiber 6g, Protein 33g, Sodium 289mg, excellent source of copper, phosphorous, zinc, vitamin A, vitamin B12

ZUCCHINI TACO BOATS

Yields 3 servings

3 medium zucchini
½ lb. organic lean ground turkey, hormone and antibiotic free
1 tbsp. chili powder
1 tsp. garlic powder
1 tbsp. ground cumin
¼ cup filtered water
Himalayan sea salt to taste
1 cup shredded Monterey jack cheese
3 cups green leaf lettuce, shredded
2 Roma tomatoes, diced
¼ cup salsa
½ cup plain Greek yogurt (10% milk-fat is best, use 2% at minimum)

Preheat oven to 375 degrees. Boil a large pot of water. Brown the turkey in a skillet and then add seasonings and ¼ cup of water, cooking down until sauce thickens. Slice each zucchini in half lengthwise and scoop out the insides leaving a ditch in each one. Blanch the zucchini in the boiling water for 2 minutes each, remove with tongs and place in glass baking dish. Stuff each boat with the ground turkey and bake for 10 minutes. Add cheese and return to oven until the cheese melts. Mix salsa and yogurt together in a bowl. Serve taco boats with diced tomatoes and lettuce, and drizzle the yogurt mixture on top.

Nutritional Information: Total Calories 344, Total Fat 17g, Carbohydrates 16g, Sugars 10g, Dietary Fiber 5g, Protein 35g, Sodium 21mg, good source of calcium, potassium, phosphorus, selenium, zinc, vitamin B6, vitamin C, and vitamin K

SPICY STEAK LETTUCE WRAPS

Yields 4 servings

1 lb. organic grass-fed sirloin steak, sliced into ½ -inch cubes
1 large yellow onion, sliced
½ cup chopped red pepper
½ cup chopped green pepper
2 green onions, sliced thin (save tops for garnish)
1 tsp. minced garlic
1 tbsp. olive oil
1 ½ tbsp. Sriracha Sauce
1 ½ tbsp. liquid aminos (soy sauce alternative)
4 large lettuce leafs (green-leaf or romaine)

Heat olive oil in skillet on high heat. Add sirloin to skillet, cook on high for 2 minutes, tossing occasionally. Add onion, peppers, green onions, and garlic and cook for 5 minutes on high, tossing occasionally. Reduce heat to medium, add Sriracha sauce and liquid aminos, cooking until sauce has been absorbed. Spoon steak mixture into lettuce leaf, garnish with sliced green onion and serve.

Nutritional Information: Total Calories 194, Total Fat 7g, Carbohydrates 7g, Sugars 4g, Dietary Fiber 2g, Protein 24g, Sodium 147mg, good source of selenium, zinc, vitamin B6, vitamin B12, and vitamin C

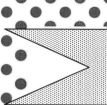

SPAGHETTI SQUASH LASAGNA

Yields 6 servings

1 lb. organic grass-fed 85% ground beef
4 lb. spaghetti squash
½ cup diced onion, fresh or frozen
1 tbsp. minced garlic
1 pint button mushrooms, sliced
15 oz. can organic no salt added diced tomatoes
6 oz. can organic tomato paste
8 oz. can organic tomato sauce
2 tbsp. Italian seasoning, divided
2 tsp. garlic powder, divided
Himalayan sea salt
½ cup filtered water
15 oz. whole milk ricotta cheese
½ cup full-fat cottage cheese
1 organic free-range egg
¼ cup parmesan cheese

Preheat the oven 350 degrees. Slice squash in half lengthwise, spoon out the seeds, sprinkle with sea salt and garlic powder and place skin side up on a rimmed baking sheet. Bake for 25 minutes until tender to touch, remove from oven and scrape out insides with a fork, layering the bottom of a 9x13 glass baking dish with the squash. Heat skillet over medium heat, add beef, onion, and minced garlic and brown meat. Add mushrooms and cook until soft, about 5 minutes. Add diced tomatoes, tomato paste, tomato sauce, 1 tbsp. Italian seasoning, 1 tsp. garlic powder, and water and let simmer on low for about 45 minutes or until thickened. Mix together ricotta cheese, cottage cheese, egg, parmesan cheese, 1 tbsp. Italian seasoning, and 1 tsp. garlic powder, stirring well to combine. Layer ricotta mixture on top of the spaghetti squash, then the meat mixture. Bake lasagna for 1 hour, remove the oven and serve.

Nutritional Information: Total Calories 414, Total Fat 21g, Carbohydrates 27g, Sugars 12g, Dietary Fiber 6g, Protein 31g, Sodium 446mg, good source of phosphorous, selenium, zinc, vitamin B6, vitamin B12, thiamin, riboflavin, and niacin

Yields 6-8 lettuce wraps

2 cups cooked and shredded organic chicken breast, hormone and antibiotic free
1 cup diced pineapple
1 cup pre-packaged broccoli slaw
½ cup slivered almonds
½ tbsp. grass-fed butter
Red-leaf lettuce (large leaves work best)
Teriyaki Sauce (see recipe next page)

To cook chicken, place chicken breast in foil piece about 1-foot long and season with sea salt, pepper, and garlic powder to taste. Wrap up tight, place on baking sheet, and bake in the oven at 375 degrees for about 40 minutes. Once chicken has cooled, shred and set aside 2 cups for recipe. Melt butter in a pan over medium heat and add almonds stirring to coat. Toast for about 1-2 minutes until almonds are a golden brown color and fragrant. Mix the chicken, pineapple, almonds, broccoli slaw, and 1 cup of the teriyaki sauce in a bowl. Chill mixture in refrigerator for at least 30 minutes. Place about ¼ cup of the chicken mixture on lettuce leaf, drizzle more teriyaki sauce on top if desired, wrap up and enjoy! There will be leftover teriyaki sauce for dipping if desired.

Teriyaki Sauce:
½ cup low sodium soy sauce
1 tbsp. raw honey
2 tbsp. brown sugar, packed
1 tsp. ground ginger
1 tsp. garlic powder
½ tsp. crushed red pepper flakes
1 cup filtered water
2 tbsp. corn starch
Himalayan sea salt to taste

Whisk together water and corn starch and set aside. Heat soy sauce, honey, brown sugar, ground ginger, garlic, sea salt, and red pepper flakes over medium heat until it reaches a simmer. Slowly whisk in corn starch and water mixture and continue to whisk until sauce thickens and is translucent.

Nutritional Information: Total Calories 157, Total Fat 7g, Carbohydrates 18g, Sugars 9g, Dietary Fiber 2g, Protein 18g, Sodium 890mg, good source of vitamin K and niacin

THAI PEANUT CHICKEN LETTUCE WRAPS

Yields 6-8 lettuce wraps

1 lb. organic boneless skinless chicken breast, antibiotic and hormone free
1 tbsp. olive oil
1 tsp. garlic powder
½ tsp. ground ginger
¼ tsp. ground red pepper
Himalayan sea salt and pepper to taste
½ cup cashews, chopped
1 cup red bell pepper, diced
2 cups pre-packaged broccoli slaw
4-6 red-leaf lettuce leaves (large leaves work best)
Thai Peanut Sauce (see recipe next page)

Slice the chicken into thin strips. Heat the olive oil in a skillet over medium-high heat, add chicken and spices and mix well to coat. Once chicken is cooked thoroughly, turn the heat down to medium and add ½ cup of the Thai Peanut Sauce and stir. Add chopped cashews and red bell pepper and toss until evenly coated. Drizzle a little of the peanut sauce on the base of the lettuce leaf, add ¼ cup of broccoli slaw, more peanut sauce and then about ½ cup of the chicken mixture. Drizzle more peanut sauce on top, roll up and serve immediately. There should be about 1 cup of leftover peanut sauce for dipping if desired. This is a great appetizer, lunch, or dinner!

Thai Peanut Sauce:
½ cup natural peanut butter
2 tbsp. low sodium soy sauce
2 tsp. rice vinegar
1 ½ tsp. ground ginger
1 tbsp. Sriracha sauce
1 tsp. garlic powder
1 tbsp. raw honey
2/3 cup unsweetened full-fat coconut milk

In a small saucepan, whisk together the peanut butter, soy sauce, ginger, garlic, vinegar, Sriracha, and honey. Whisk in coconut milk last. Heat over medium-low heat for 1-2 minutes, adding more coconut milk as needed if the sauce becomes too thick. The sauce should drip steadily off of a spoon.

Nutritional Information: Total Calories 180, Total Fat 13g, Carbohydrates 6g, Sugars 3g, Dietary Fiber 2g, Protein 18g, Sodium 327mg, excellent source of vitamin C

CHICKEN STUFFED PORTABELLAS

Yields 6 servings

6 large portabella mushroom caps
1 ½ lb. organic boneless skinless chicken breast, hormone and antibiotic free
1 cup wild rice, cooked
1 large yellow or orange bell pepper, diced
1 medium red onion, diced
1 tbsp. minced garlic
1 tbsp. clarified butter (ghee)
½ tbsp. olive oil
½ tsp. garlic powder
½ tsp. onion powder
1 tsp. dried thyme
Himalayan sea salt and pepper to taste

Preheat the oven to 350 degrees. Clean mushrooms, remove stems and dry with a paper towel. Brush tops of mushroom caps with olive oil and sprinkle with garlic powder, onion powder, sea salt, and black pepper. Place on rimmed baking sheet gill side up and bake for approximately 10 minutes. Pound chicken into ½-inch thick pieces and slice into ½-inch cubes. Heat the ghee in a skillet over medium-high heat, add minced garlic and red onion and cook for 2-3 minutes. Add bell peppers, garlic powder, onion powder, thyme, and chicken and sauté until chicken is cooked through. Add cooked wild rice and stir. Stuff each mushroom with a rounded ½ cup of the rice mixture, forming a mound. Place mushrooms on rimmed baking sheet and bake for 10 minutes, heating thoroughly. Serve immediately with a mixed greens salad on the side.

Nutritional Information: Total Calories 254, Total Fat 7g, Carbohydrates 19g, Sugars 3g, Dietary Fiber 3g, Protein 30g, Sodium 72mg, excellent source of selenium, vitamin B6, vitamin C, vitamin D, and niacin

ITLAIAN CHICKEN VEGETABLE SOUP

Yields 4 servings

1 lb. organic boneless skinless chicken breast, hormone and antibiotic free, cubed
2 slices uncured, nitrate/nitrite free bacon, crumbled
12 oz. bag frozen butternut squash, or 2 cups fresh butternut squash cubed
2 medium organic carrots, sliced into ¼ -inch pieces
2 medium parsnips, sliced into ¼ -inch pieces
2 organic celery ribs, sliced into ¼ -inch pieces
1 tbsp. fresh parsley leaves
1 tbsp. minced garlic
1 small onion, diced
2 cups organic kale, chopped
4 cups organic low-sodium chicken stock (look for gluten free)
6 oz. can organic tomato paste
2 tsp. Italian seasoning
Himalayan sea salt and pepper to taste
¼ tsp. red pepper flakes
2 tbsp. olive oil
1 tbsp. grass-fed butter
Parmesan cheese (optional)

Cook bacon in a skillet over medium heat until crispy, set aside on a paper towel. Heat olive oil and butter in large stock pot on medium heat, add chicken and cook until no longer pink. Add onion, minced garlic and cook until translucent. Add carrots, celery, and parsnips, cooking for about 5 minutes. Add chicken stock, tomato paste, Italian seasoning, red pepper flakes, salt and pepper, stirring until well blended. Simmer on medium heat about 20 minutes and add butternut squash and kale, simmer an additional 10 minutes or until vegetables are tender. Serve soup immediately topped with fresh parsley leaves, crumbled bacon, and Parmesan cheese

Nutritional Information: Total Calories 260, Total Fat 6g, Carbohydrates 19g, Sugars 4g, Dietary Fiber 3g, Protein 34g, Sodium 238mg, excellent source of copper, vitamin A, vitamin B6, vitamin C, vitamin K, and niacin

BACON WRAPPED CHICKEN TENDERS

Yields 6 chicken tenders

1 lb. organic chicken tenders, antibiotic and hormone free
¼ cup olive oil
¼ cup Sriracha sauce
¼ cup raw honey
1 tsp. garlic powder
Himalayan sea salt and pepper to taste
6 slices uncured, nitrate/nitrite free bacon

Whisk together olive oil, Sriracha, garlic powder, salt, pepper, and honey. Marinate chicken in sauce for 30 minutes in the refrigerator. Remove chicken from sauce and wrap each piece with a slice of bacon. Line a baking sheet with parchment paper and place chicken tenders on sheet, pouring the excess sauce on top. Bake at 375 degrees for about 25 minutes. Serve with avocado sauce (see Snacks, Dips, and Spreads section) or enjoy plain!

Nutritional Information: Total Calories 405, Total Fat 20g, Carbohydrates 15g, Sugars 13g, Dietary Fiber 1g, Protein 41g, Sodium 495mg, excellent source of phosphorous, selenium, vitamin B6, and niacin

CHICKEN CURRY

Yields 4 servings

1 lb. organic boneless skinless chicken breast, antibiotic and hormone free, cut into cubes
2 cups basmati rice, cooked
1 cup unsweetened full-fat coconut milk
14.5 oz. can organic, no salt added diced tomatoes, drained well
2 tsp. minced garlic
¼ cup green onion, sliced thin
2 tbsp. olive oil, divided
2 tsp. curry powder
¼ tsp. cayenne pepper
1 tsp. ground coriander
½ tsp. ground turmeric
¼ tsp. ground ginger
¼ tsp. Himalayan sea salt
¼ ground black pepper

Heat 1 tbsp. of the olive oil in medium size skillet on medium heat, add chicken and cook until no longer pink, remove from skillet and set aside. In the same skillet, heat the rest of the olive oil, add garlic and onion, and cook for 2 minutes, tossing occasionally. In a small bowl combine spices and mix well. Add spice mixture to skillet with tomatoes, cook for 2 minutes, tossing occasionally. Stir in coconut milk, bring to a boil then reduce heat. Add chicken back to skillet and cook for about 5 minutes. Serve over ½ cup of basmati rice.

Nutritional Information: Total Calories 463, Total Fat 25g, Carbohydrates 31g, Sugars 5g, Dietary Fiber 3g, Protein 30g, Sodium 161mg, excellent source of selenium and niacin

ZUCCHINI CHICKEN ALFREDO

Yields 5 servings

1 lb. organic boneless skinless chicken breast, antibiotic and hormone free, sliced into strips
4 slices uncured, nitrate/nitrite free bacon
3 large zucchini, spiraled (use a grater if you do not have a spiralizer)
2 tbsp. grass-fed butter
1 tbsp. minced garlic
1 tbsp. garlic powder
1 tsp. onion powder
Himalayan sea salt to taste
¼ cup white cooking wine
1 tsp. corn starch
½ cup grated parmesan cheese
13.6 oz. can unsweetened full-fat coconut milk

Boil a large pot of water. Meanwhile, cook bacon in a skillet until crispy. Remove bacon and place on paper towel, then cook chicken in the same skillet with the bacon grease until cooked through, seasoning with salt and pepper. Remove chicken and set aside. Melt butter in skillet over medium-high heat and add minced garlic and cook until it browns. Add coconut milk, spices, cooking wine, and corn starch. Mix in parmesan cheese and let cook for 3-4 minutes and turn heat to low to keep warm. Crush bacon into pieces and add it to the Alfredo sauce. Blanch spiraled zucchini in boiling water for 2-3 minutes, remove and drain excess water. Plate zucchini and add sauce and chicken on top. Serve immediately.

Nutritional Information: Total Calories 471, Total Fat 32g, Carbohydrates 11g, Sugars 6g, Dietary Fiber 3g, Protein 36g, Sodium 648mg, excellent source of phosphorous, selenium, vitamin B6, and niacin

WHITE CHICKEN CHILI

Yields 6 servings

1 lb. organic, lean ground chicken or turkey breast, hormone and antibiotic free
½ cup chopped onion, fresh or frozen
1 tbsp. minced garlic
2 -15 oz. cans great northern beans or cannellini beans (white kidney beans)
7 oz. can chopped green chilies
2 cups low sodium chicken broth (look for gluten free)
1 tsp. Better Than Bouillon chicken base
1 tbsp. ground cumin
2 tsp. oregano
1 tsp. ground cayenne or red pepper (optional for extra spice)
½ tsp. ground pepper
Himalayan sea salt to taste

Heat skillet over medium heat and brown ground turkey or chicken until cooked thoroughly. Add onions and garlic and cook until tender. Rinse and drain beans, add to skillet with chilies, chicken broth, chicken base, cumin, oregano, cayenne pepper, pepper, and salt. Simmer on low heat for 1 hour and 30 minutes or until liquid has reduced and thickened (do not boil). Serve with Mexican shredded cheese and 1 tbsp. of Greek yogurt if desired.

Nutritional Information: Total Calories 321, Total Fat 3g, Carbohydrates 42g, Sugars 2g, Dietary Fiber 11g, Protein 33g, Sodium 239mg, excellent source of copper, phosphorous, vitamin B6, and niacin

SAGE CHICKEN AND FALL HARVEST VEGETABLES

Yields 6 servings

2 lb. organic chicken breast, hormone and antibiotic free
2 medium yellow onions, sliced
½ cup organic, low-sodium chicken broth
12 oz. bag organic diced butternut squash
2 small sweet potatoes, cubed
¼ cup apple cider vinegar
1 tbsp. dried sage
½ tbsp. dried rosemary
½ tsp. ground cinnamon

Place onions and potatoes into the bottom of a crockpot. Add chicken, spices, vinegar, and broth. Cook on high for 3 hours, adding the squash for the last 20 minutes of cooking.

Nutritional Information: Total Calories 254, Total Fat 4g, Carbohydrates 17g, Sugars 4g, Dietary Fiber 3g, Protein 36g, Sodium 110mg, excellent source of selenium, vitamin A, vitamin B6, and niacin

CHICKEN FAJITA BAKE

Yields 6 servings

1 lb. organic boneless, skinless chicken breasts, antibiotic and hormone free, cut into strips
2 cups organic baby spinach
3 bell peppers, cut into strips
1 sweet yellow onion, cut into strips
1 pint button mushrooms with stems, sliced
¼ cup sliced jalapenos, jarred or fresh
2 tbsp. olive oil
1 tbsp. chili powder
1 tsp. garlic powder
1 tbsp. ground cumin
½ tsp. Himalayan pink sea salt
Optional: ½ cup Monterey jack cheese, shredded

Preheat oven to 375 degrees. Drizzle olive oil into the bottom of a 9x13 glass casserole dish. Layer onions, peppers, spinach, jalapenos, mushrooms, spinach, chicken, and seasonings. Bake for 40-45 minutes until chicken is cooked through. If topping with cheese, remove after 30 minutes, top with cheese and return to the oven to bake for an additional 10 minutes. Serve immediately.

Nutritional Information (without cheese): Total Calories 149, Total Fat 5g, Carbohydrates 8g, Sugars 3g, Dietary Fiber 3g, Protein 19g, Sodium 302mg, excellent source of vitamin C, vitamin k, and niacin

CHICKEN SPINACH ARTICHOKE BAKE

Yields 6 servings

2 lbs. organic boneless skinless chicken breast, hormone and antibiotic free, cut into ½-inch cubes
14 oz. can artichoke hearts, drained
1 pint button mushrooms, sliced
2 cups organic baby spinach leaves
½ cup unsweetened full-fat coconut milk
2 tsp. garlic powder
½ tbsp. dried oregano
½ tbsp. dried basil
Himalayan sea salt and pepper to taste

Preheat oven to 350 degrees. Layer cubed chicken in bottom of 9x13 glass baking dish, add 1 tsp. of garlic, and salt and pepper to taste. Layer with spinach leaves, mushrooms, artichokes, 1 tsp. of garlic powder, basil, oregano, and coconut milk. Bake uncovered for 35-40 minutes or until chicken is cooked thoroughly. Serve immediately.

Nutritional Information: Total Calories 270, Total Fat 9g, Carbohydrates 10g, Sugars 2g, Dietary Fiber 6g, Protein 38g, Sodium 162mg, excellent source of phosphorous, selenium, vitamin B6, vitamin K, and niacin

LEMON DILL SALMON

Yields 4 servings

4, 5 oz. wild-caught salmon fillets
8 tbsp. grass-fed butter
1 tbsp. olive oil
½ cup fresh lemon juice (about 2 lemons)
1 tsp. minced garlic
¼ oz. fresh dill (or 1 tsp. dried dill)
2 tsp. corn starch
Himalayan sea salt and pepper to taste

Heat butter and olive oil in a skillet over medium-high heat until it bubbles. Add lemon juice, garlic, and dill and bring to a boil. Add corn starch and whisk until sauce thickens. Place salmon fillets in skillet and cook for about 3 minutes on each side, until fish flakes apart. Serve with fresh lemon juice and lemon slice for garnish.

Nutritional Information: Total Calories 445, Total Fat 34g, Carbohydrates 2g, Sugars 0g, Dietary Fiber 0g, Protein 31g, Sodium 204mg, excellent source of phosphorous, vitamin B6, vitamin B12, vitamin D, and niacin

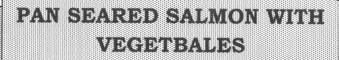

Yields 8 servings

Salmon:
8 wild-caught skinless salmon fillets
2 ½ tbsp. paprika
2 tbsp. Himalayan sea salt
2 tbsp. garlic powder
1 tbsp. black pepper
1 tbsp. onion powder
1 tbsp. cayenne pepper
1 tbsp. dried oregano
1 tbsp. dried thyme
olive oil for cookinG

Combine all spices in a bowl and season salmon generously. Store extra seasoning in a jar or air-tight container. Heat skillet with oil and cook salmon on each side for 2-3 minutes.

Vegetables:
1 yellow onion, sliced
3 bell peppers, sliced
2 medium zucchini, spiraled (use grater if you don't have a spiralizer)
1 pint button mushrooms, sliced
4 cups organic baby spinach
1 jar marinated quartered artichoke hearts, drained
¼ cup Kalamata olives
Himalayan sea salt and pepper to taste
olive oil for cooking

Heat oil in a skillet over medium-high heat. Add vegetables and cook until al dente or to desired tenderness.

Nutritional Information: Total Calories 384, Total Fat 20g, Carbohydrates 16g, Sugars 4g, Dietary Fiber 9g, Protein 37g, Sodium 423mg, excellent source of vitamin B6 and B12, vitamin C, vitamin D, vitamin K, niacin, phosphorus, and selenium

LEMON PEPPER COD

Yields 4 servings

4, 4-6 oz. wild-caught cod fillets
2 tbsp. olive oil
1 tbsp. minced garlic
1 tbsp. lemon pepper seasoning
1 large lemon, cut in half
green onion for garnish

Heat olive oil in skillet over medium-high heat, add minced garlic and brown for 1-2 minutes. Add cod fillets to skillet, squeeze lemon juice from ½ of the lemon over the fish, season with lemon pepper and cook for about 2-3 minutes on each side. Once fish flakes apart, remove from heat and serve with green onion and lemon slices.

Nutritional Information: Total Calories 158, Total Fat 7g, Carbohydrates 1g, Sugars 0g, Dietary Fiber 0g, Protein 21g, Sodium 83mg, good source of vitamin B6

Yields 2 servings (2 tacos per serving)

Shrimp Tacos:

1 lb. raw large shrimp, peeled and deveined
2 tbsp. freshly squeezed lime juice
2 tbsp. olive oil
2 tbsp. fresh cilantro, minced
1 tsp. ground cumin
½ tsp. smoked paprika
½ tsp. garlic powder
Himalayan sea salt and pepper to taste
4-6 whole wheat tortillas

Combine lime juice, olive oil, cilantro, cumin, paprika, garlic powder, salt, and pepper in a medium size bowl, mix well. Add shrimp and marinate in the refrigerator for 30 minutes. While shrimp marinates prepare mango salsa and avocado sauce.

Mango Salsa:

2 large mangos, peeled, pitted and finely diced
½ cup red bell pepper, finely diced
¼ cup red onion, finely diced
1 medium lime, juiced
1 tbsp. fresh cilantro, minced
Himalayan sea salt to taste

Combine mangos, red bell pepper, red onion, lime juice, cilantro, salt in pepper into small bowl, mix thoroughly. Refrigerate for 30 minutes.

Avocado Sauce:

1 large avocado
½ cup plain Greek yogurt (10% milk-fat is best, use 2% at minimum)
1 medium lime, juiced
½ tsp. garlic powder
Himalayan sea salt and pepper to taste

Combine avocado, yogurt, lime juice, garlic powder, salt, and pepper into food processor or blender and blend until smooth. Transfer to small bowl and refrigerate for 30 minutes.

Cook shrimp mixture in medium size skillet on medium-high heat until shrimp is thoroughly cooked and pink in color. Spoon cooked shrimp into whole wheat tortilla and top with mango salsa and avocado sauce. Serve immediately.

Nutritional Information (without toppings): Total Calories 478, Total Fat 21g, Carbohydrates 136g, Sugars 2g, Dietary Fiber 2g, Protein 36g, Sodium 650mg,

SPAGHETTI SQUASH SHRIMP SCAMPI

Yields 4 servings

2 lb. spaghetti squash
1 lb. jumbo shrimp, peeled, and deveined
1 tbsp. minced garlic
1 large lemon, juiced
1 large lemon, quartered
2 tbsp. olive oil
2 tbsp. grass-fed butter
½ tsp. dried lemon peel
1 ½ tsp. dried oregano
1 tsp. dried basil
½ tsp. red pepper flakes
Himalayan seat salt and pepper to taste

Preheat the oven to 350 degrees. Cut spaghetti squash in half, remove seeds with a spoon and place skin side up on a baking sheet. Bake for 20-25 minutes until squash pulls apart easily with a fork. While squash is cooking, heat the butter and 1 tbsp. of the olive oil in a skillet over medium-high heat. Add minced garlic, shrimp, red pepper flakes, ½ tsp. of dried oregano, lemon juice, lemon peel, sea salt and pepper and cook until shrimp are cooked thoroughly and pink in color. Remove from heat and set aside. Remove squash from the oven, scoop out the inside of the squash and transfer to a bowl. Add 1 tbsp. of the olive oil, 1 tsp. of oregano, basil, sea salt, and pepper to the squash, tossing to combine. Plate spaghetti squash, top with sautéed shrimp and squeeze juice from ¼ lemon over each plate. Serve immediately.

Nutritional Information: Total Calories 229, Total Fat 14g, Carbohydrates 10g, Sugars 3g, Dietary Fiber 2g, Protein 16g, Sodium 220mg, good source of phosphorous and vitamin B12

Yields 4 servings

1 lb. cooked jumbo shrimp, peeled and deveined
2 cups basmati rice, cooked
1 cup unsweetened full-fat coconut milk
14.5 oz. can organic, no salt added diced tomatoes, drained well
2 tsp. minced garlic
¼ cup green onion
1 tbsp. olive oil
2 tsp. curry powder
¼ tsp. cayenne pepper
1 tsp. ground coriander
½ tsp. ground turmeric
¼ tsp. ground ginger
¼ tsp. Himalayan sea salt
¼ ground black pepper

Heat olive oil in medium size skillet on medium heat, add garlic and onion, and cook for 2 minutes, tossing occasionally. In a small bowl combine spices and mix well. Add spice mixture to skillet with tomatoes, cook for 2 minutes, tossing occasionally. Stir in coconut milk, bring to a boil then reduce heat. Add shrimp and cook for about 5 minutes. Serve over ½ cup of basmati rice.

Nutritional Information: Total Calories 378, Total Fat 19g, Carbohydrates 33g, Sugars 5g, Dietary Fiber 4g, Protein 20g, Sodium 250mg, excellent source of copper and selenium

SHRIMP STUFFED PORTABELLA MUSHROOMS

Yields 6 servings

6 large portabella mushroom caps
1 lb. shrimp, raw, peeled, and deveined
1 cup wild rice, cooked
1 yellow or orange bell pepper, diced
½ red onion, diced
1 tbsp. minced garlic
1 tbsp. olive oil
1 tbsp. clarified butter (ghee)
½ tsp. garlic powder
½ tsp. onion powder
1 tsp. dried thyme
Himalayan sea salt and pepper to taste

Preheat the oven to 350 degrees. Clean mushrooms, remove stems and dry with a paper towel. Brush tops of mushroom caps with olive oil and sprinkle with garlic powder, onion powder, sea salt, and black pepper. Place on rimmed baking sheet gill side up and bake for approximately 10 minutes. Heat the olive oil and butter in a skillet over medium-high heat; add minced garlic and brown, about 2 minutes. Add onion powder and garlic powder and stir. Add shrimp and sauté until cooked thoroughly and pink in color. Add thyme, sea salt, and pepper, stirring to combine. Once shrimp are cooked, remove from skillet and dice into small pieces. Add more olive oil to the skillet if needed and add the diced bell pepper and red onion. Sauté for 2-3 minutes then add cooked wild rice and stir. Remove from heat and combine rice mixture with the diced shrimp in a bowl. Add additional salt to taste and combine mixture thoroughly. Stuff each mushroom with approximately ½ cup of the shrimp, rice, and pepper mixture, forming a mound. Place mushrooms on rimmed baking sheet and bake for 10 minutes, heating thoroughly. Serve immediately with a mixed greens salad on the side.

Nutritional Information: Total Calories 224, Total Fat 6g, Carbohydrates 28g, Sugars 3g, Dietary Fiber 3g, Protein 16g, Sodium 435mg

Yields 5 servings

1 ½ lb. pork tenderloin
1 tbsp. olive oil
¼ cup filtered water
¼ cup apple cider vinegar
¼ cup 100% apple juice concentrate

Sweet and Spicy Rub:
1 tbsp. chipotle powder
1 tbsp. ground coriander
2 tbsp. garlic powder
3 tbsp. onion powder
1 tbsp. dried oregano
1 tbsp. dried thyme
1 tbsp. ground black pepper
6 tbsp. brown sugar
2 tbsp. chili powder
3 tbsp. sea salt
1 tsp. ground cinnamon
1 tbsp. ground nutmeg
3 tbsp. paprika
2 tbsp. smoked paprika
1 tbsp. ground ginger
* This will make more rub than you will need, store additional rub in glass container.

Mix together spices in a small bowl until well blended, set aside.

Preheat the oven to 220 degrees. Rub pork loin with olive oil, coating well. Place pork loin in 15" oval roasting pan and coat with spice rub, covering generously. Add water, apple juice, and apple vinegar to the roaster. Cook uncovered for 2 hours. Remove from oven and set aside to cool, slice thinly and serve immediately.

Nutritional Information: Total Calories 163, Total Fat 6g, Carbohydrates 5g, Sugars 5g, Dietary Fiber 0g, Protein 21g, Sodium 512mg

Yields 8 servings

2 lb. pork loin, antibiotic and hormone free, butterflied

1 lb. uncured, nitrate/nitrite free bacon

12 oz. jar roasted red peppers, drained and sliced

3 oz. crumbled full-fat feta cheese

8.5 oz. jar sun-dried tomatoes (will only use half of the jar)

2 cups organic baby spinach

¼ cup Kalamata olive spread

10-12 fresh basil leaves, stems removed

1 tbsp. dried basil

1 tsp. garlic powder

1 tbsp. dried oregano

½ tsp. Himalayan sea salt

Preheat the oven to 375 degrees. Mix together dried spices in a small bowl and set aside. Butterfly the pork tenderloin and pound with mallet. Spread the Kalamata olive spread onto the pork tenderloin, then layer on the spinach and fresh basil leaves, roasted red peppers, sun-dried tomatoes, feta cheese, and ½ of the spice mix. Roll it up, then cover with bacon and use toothpicks to keep it all together, use as many as you need. Use the other half of the spice mix to coat the outside of the pork. Place in a casserole dish and bake until the meat reaches 160 degrees, about 30-40 minutes.

Nutritional Information: Total Calories 242, Total Fat 12g, Carbohydrates 5g, Sugars 3g, Dietary Fiber 1g, Protein 29g, Sodium 822mg

SWEET POTATO SAUSAGE SKILLET

Yields 4 servings

4 dinner chicken sausages, antibiotic, hormone, and nitrate/nitrite free
2 medium sweet potatoes, peeled and cut into ¼-inch cubes
½ cup white onion, diced (fresh or frozen)
1 medium red onion, diced
½ cup green pepper, diced (fresh or frozen)
¼ cup jarred sliced jalapenos
2 tsp. minced garlic
2 tbsp. olive oil
1 tsp. ground cumin
½ tsp. garlic powder
¼ tsp. ground chipotle chili powder
Himalayan sea salt and black pepper to taste

In a medium size pot, bring water to boil, add sweet potatoes and boil for 6-8 minutes. Drain the water and set aside to dry. In medium size skillet heat 1 tbsp. olive oil on medium-high heat, add onions and peppers, stirring often and cooking until onions become translucent. Remove cooked peppers and onions, set aside on plate. Add remaining olive oil to pan and add sweet potatoes, green peppers, onions, jalapenos, garlic, cumin, chipotle chili powder, salt and pepper, making a single layer. Cook mixture until potatoes are browned, stirring occasionally. Remove mixture from skillet and set aside. Slice chicken sausages at an angle, brown in skillet on medium-high heat. Portion potato mixture onto plate and top with chicken sausage slices.

Nutritional Information: Total Calories 284, Total Fat 14g, Carbohydrates 25g, Sugars 9g, Dietary Fiber 1g, Protein 16g, Sodium 635mg, good source of manganese, vitamin A, and vitamin C

STUFFED MUSHROOMS WITH BLUEBERRY GLAZE

Yields 4 servings

4 large portabella mushroom caps
15 oz. whole milk ricotta cheese
1 tsp. minced garlic
1 ½ tsp. dried basil
1 ½ tsp. dried oregano
12 oz. jar roasted red peppers
4 oz. crumbled blue cheese
organic baby spinach leaves
Himalayan sea salt to taste

Blueberry Balsamic Glaze:
1 pint organic blueberries
½ cup balsamic vinegar
1 tbsp. corn starch
2 tbsp. natural grape jelly, no preservatives or high fructose corn syrup

Preheat oven to 375 degrees. Combine blueberries, corn starch, balsamic vinegar and corn starch in a blender or food processor until well blended. Transfer to a small saucepan and heat on medium until warm. Brush outside of mushroom caps with olive oil and place gill side up on a rimmed baking sheet lined with foil. Mix ricotta cheese, minced garlic, oregano, basil, and sea salt in a bowl. Layer each mushroom with ¼ cup of the ricotta mixture. Place 1-2 red peppers and a few spinach leaves on each mushroom. Layer each mushroom again with ricotta mixture. Dice leftover red peppers, about ½ cup, and top each mushroom with the red peppers and blue cheese crumbles. Bake for 20 minutes and serve immediately with blueberry balsamic glaze drizzled on top.

Nutritional Information: Total Calories 365, Total Fat 23g, Carbohydrates 19g, Sugars 10g, Dietary Fiber 2g, Protein 21g, Sodium 504mg, good source of manganese, vitamin A, and vitamin C, good source of calcium, copper, selenium, phosphorous, vitamin C, vitamin D, and riboflavin

- BACON WRAPPED JALAPENO BITES (GF, EF)

- RED PEPPER HUMMUS (GF, EF)

- RED PEPPER HUMMUS PINWHEELS (GF, DF, EF)

- MANGO SALSA (GF, DF, EF)

- GUACAMOLE (GF, DF, EF)

- PUMPKIN YOGURT (GF, EF)

- AVOCADO SAUCE (GF, EF)

- TERIYAKI SAUCE (GF, EF)

- THAI PEANUT SAUCE (DF, EF)

- TACO SEASONING MIX (GF, DF, EF)

BACON WRAPPED JALAPENO BITES

Yields 16 bite-sized pieces (4 pieces is one serving)

8 jalapeno peppers
1 lb. organic grass-fed 85% ground beef
1 lb. uncured, nitrate/nitrite free bacon
¼ cup shredded Monterey jack cheese
1 tbsp. ground cumin
1 tbsp. chili powder
2 tsp. garlic powder
¼ tsp. Himalayan sea salt

Preheat the oven to 375 degrees. Slice jalapenos in half and remove seeds. Place on a baking sheet lined with parchment paper and set aside. Brown meat in a skillet and add the seasonings with ¼ cup of filtered water. When the water cooks down and the sauce thickens, spoon some of the beef mixture into each jalapeno. Wrap each one with a piece of bacon and use toothpicks to secure if necessary. Bake for 20 minutes or until bacon is crispy. Sprinkle with cheese and return to the oven for 2 minutes. Serve immediately.

Nutritional Information: Total Calories 311, Total Fat 20g, Carbohydrates 5g, Sugars 2g, Dietary Fiber 1g, Protein 28g, Sodium 626mg, excellent source of vitamin B12, vitamin C, and zinc. Also a good source of phosphorus, selenium, and iron

RED PEPPER HUMMUS

Yields 12 servings (¼ cup servings)

2 15 oz. cans of chickpeas or garbanzo beans, drained
1 large red pepper, chopped
3 tbsp. tahini
1 tbsp. olive oil
3 tbsp. lemon juice, fresh squeezed
½ tsp. ground cumin
½ tsp. Himalayan sea salt
½ tsp. garlic powder

Add all ingredients into food processor or blender. Blend on medium speed until red pepper is evenly distributed. Transfer hummus into glass container and refrigerate for 2 hours until chilled. Serve with fresh vegetables.

Nutritional Information: Total Calories 101, Total Fat 5g, Carbohydrates 12g, Sugars 3g, Dietary Fiber 4g, Protein 4g, Sodium 196mg

RED PEPPER HUMMUS PINWHEELS

Yields 20 pinwheels (4 pinwheels is one serving)

2 straight cucumbers or zucchini, medium size
½ cup red pepper hummus (see previous recipe)
¼ cup crumbled full-fat feta cheese
Optional: diced roasted red peppers

Slice cucumber or zucchini into long strips using vegetable peeler or mandoline. Spread small amount of hummus onto each cucumber or zucchini strip, sprinkle with feta cheese and diced peppers. Roll cucumber or zucchini into a tight roll and secure with a toothpick. Refrigerate for 30 minutes and serve.

Nutritional Information: Total Calories 70, Total Fat 4g, Carbohydrates 7g, Sugars 2g, Dietary Fiber 2g, Protein 3g, Sodium 164mg

MANGO SALSA

Yields 8 servings (½ cup servings)

2 large mangos, peeled, pitted and finely diced
½ cup red bell pepper, finely diced
¼ cup red onion, finely diced
1 medium lime, juiced
1 tbsp. fresh cilantro, minced
Himalayan sea salt to taste

Combine mangoes, red bell pepper, red onion, lime juice, cilantro, and sea salt. Refrigerate for at least 30 minutes before serving.

Nutritional Information: Total Calories 40, Total Fat 0g, Carbohydrates 10g, Sugars 8g, Dietary Fiber 1g, Protein 0g, Sodium 21mg, good source of vitamin C

Yields 12 servings (¼ cup servings)

3 ripe avocados, pitted and skin removed
2 Roma tomatoes, diced
1 tbsp. garlic powder
1 tsp. Himalayan sea salt
1 medium lime, juiced

Mash avocados in a bowl with a fork, add garlic, sea salt, and lime juice and mix well. Add tomatoes and stir to combine, then taste and adjust seasonings as desired. Good for dipping vegetables like peppers, celery, carrots, or bean chips.

Nutritional Information: Total Calories 60, Total Fat 5g, Carbohydrates 4g, Sugars 1g, Dietary Fiber 2g, Protein 1g, Sodium 197mg

PUMPKIN YOGURT

Yields 4 servings

2 cups plain Greek yogurt (10% milk-fat is best, use 2% at minimum)
¾ cup pumpkin puree (not pumpkin pie filling)
1 tbsp. ground cinnamon
½ tbsp. pumpkin pie spice
Optional: stevia to taste

Combine all ingredients with a hand mixer. Refrigerate overnight. Sprinkle with pumpkin pie spice for serving if desired.

Nutritional Information: Total Calories 175, Total Fat 11g, Carbohydrates 11g, Sugars 4g, Dietary Fiber 3g, Protein 9g, Sodium 57mg, excellent source of vitamin A

AVOCADO SAUCE

Yields about 1 cup (2 tbsp. is one serving)

1 large avocado
½ cup plain Greek yogurt (10% milk-fat is best, use 2% at lowest)
1 medium lime, juiced
½ tsp. garlic powder
Himalayan sea salt and pepper to taste

Combine avocado, yogurt, lime juice, garlic powder, salt and pepper into food processor or blender, blend until smooth. Transfer to small bowl and refrigerate for 30 minutes.

Nutritional Information: Total Calories 52, Total Fat 4g, Carbohydrates 4g, Sugars 0g, Dietary Fiber 2g, Protein 1g, Sodium 30mg

TERIYAKI SAUCE

Yields about 1 ½ cups

½ cup low sodium soy sauce
1 tbsp. raw honey
2 tbsp. brown sugar, packed
1 tsp. ground ginger
1 tsp. garlic powder
½ tsp. crushed red pepper flakes
1 cup filtered water
2 tbsp. corn starch
Himalayan sea salt to taste

Whisk together water and corn starch and set aside. Heat soy sauce, honey, brown sugar, ground ginger, garlic, sea salt, and red pepper flakes over medium heat until it reaches a simmer. Slowly whisk in corn starch and water mixture and continue to whisk until sauce thickens and is translucent. This is a great sauce to use for lettuce wraps!

Nutritional Information (per ¼ cup): Total Calories 47, Total Fat 0g, Carbohydrates 11g, Sugars 6g, Dietary Fiber 0g, Protein 1g, Sodium 710mg

Yields about 2 cups

½ cup natural peanut butter
2 tbsp. low sodium soy sauce
2 tsp. rice vinegar
1 ½ tsp. ground ginger
1 tbsp. Sriracha sauce
1 tsp. garlic powder
1 tbsp. raw honey
2/3 cup unsweetened full-fat coconut milk

In a small saucepan, whisk together the peanut butter, soy sauce, ginger, garlic, vinegar, Sriracha, and honey. Whisk in coconut milk last. Heat over medium-low heat for 1-2 minutes, adding more coconut milk as needed if the sauce becomes too thick. The sauce should drip steadily off of a spoon. Use as a dipping sauce for raw vegetables, salad dressing, or for lettuce wraps.

Nutritional Information (per ¼ cup): Total Calories 136, Total Fat 11g, Carbohydrates 6g, Sugars 3g, Dietary Fiber 1g, Protein 4g, Sodium 192mg

Yields ½ cup of seasoning

2 tbsp. chili powder
1 tbsp. ground cumin
½ tbsp. dried oregano leaves
2 tsp. garlic powder
2 tsp. onion powder
½ tsp. crushed red pepper flakes
½ tsp. Himalayan sea salt
½ tsp. ground black pepper

Mix seasonings together in small bowl until well blended. Use for Mexican dishes instead of the processed seasoning packets. Mix seasoning in Plain Greek yogurt for a delicious dip and serve with vegetable slices for a healthy snack. Store in air tight container or jar.

DESSERTS

- BAKED PEACH COBBLER (GF, DF, EF)

- BLACK CHERRY WALNUT STUFFED PEARS (GF, EF)

- CHOCOLATE ALMOND BUTTER CUPS (EF)

- COCONUT ALMOND BUTTER BITES (GF, DF, EF)

- STRAWBERRY SHORTCAKE PROTEIN BALLS (EF)

- APPLE CINNAMON MUFFINS (GF)

- STRAWBERRY CHEESECAKE BITES (EF)

- PUMPKIN PIE BITES (EF)

- PUMPKIN CHOCOLATE CHIP COOKIES

- PUMPKIN CHEESECAKE SQUARES

- CHOCOLATE AVOCADO MOUSSE (GF, EF)

BAKED PEACH COBBLER

Yields 4 servings (½ peach is 1 serving)

2 organic white peaches
¼ cup natural almond butter
½ cup unsweetened full-fat coconut milk
2 tbsp. unsweetened coconut flakes
½ tsp. stevia extract
½ tsp. ground cinnamon

Preheat oven to 375 degrees. Slice peaches in half and remove pits. Place in a small baking dish. Spread 1 tbsp. almond butter inside each peach half. Sprinkle with cinnamon, stevia, and ½ tbsp. of coconut flakes. Bake in the oven for 15 minutes. Remove baking dish from oven, pour coconut milk on top of peaches and place back in the oven, baking an additional 10-15 minutes. Serve immediately with ½ cup of blueberry muesli (see breakfast section)

Nutritional Information: Total Calories 211, Total Fat 18g, Carbohydrates 13g, Sugars 8g, Dietary Fiber 3g, Protein 4g, Sodium 77mg, good source of copper and vitamin E

BLACK CHERRY WALNUT STUFFED PEARS

Yields 4 servings

2 organic pears, halved and pitted
¼ cup dried cherries, finely chopped
¼ cup walnuts, finely chopped
1 tbsp. raw honey
½ tsp. ground cinnamon
2 tbsp. grass-fed butter

Preheat oven to 350 degrees. Slice a small piece off the bottom of each pear so it will sit upright in baking dish. Sprinkle cinnamon over pears in baking dish. Mix cherries and walnuts together, spoon 2 tbsp. of mixture into each pear center. Drizzle honey over each pear and top with ½ tbsp. of butter and bake for 20 minutes or until easily poked with a fork.

Nutritional Information: Total Calories 198, Total Fat 11g, Carbohydrates 26g, Sugars 19g, Dietary Fiber 4g, Protein 2g, Sodium 3mg

CHOCOLATE ALMOND BUTTER CUPS

Yields 14 almond butter cups (1 cup is one serving)

1 cup creamy natural almond butter
1 cup unsweetened coconut flakes
1 tbsp. coconut oil
1 tsp. vanilla extract
12 oz. bag dark chocolate chips, at least 70% cocoa
Himalayan sea salt

Combine almond butter, vanilla, and coconut flakes in an electric mixer or with a hand mixer. Place mixture in the freezer to let it set. Melt chocolate using a double broiler with 1 tbsp. of coconut oil. Line the bottom of silicone muffin cups (or use a regular muffin tin with paper holders) with 1 tsp. of the chocolate using a teaspoon scooper and let set in the freezer for about 15 minutes. Use a teaspoon scooper to spoon the almond butter mixture into each muffin cup and cover with 1 tsp. of chocolate. Sprinkle with Himalayan sea salt and place back into the freezer for at least 25 minutes or until set. Store in freezer or refrigerator.

* you will have approximately 1/2 cup of the almond butter mixture left over to make Coconut Almond Butter Bites (see next recipe)

Nutritional Information: Total Calories 274, Total Fat 22g, Carbohydrates 19g, Sugars 13g, Dietary Fiber 3g, Protein 4g, Sodium 99mg, good source of magnesium

COCONUT ALMOND BUTTER BITES

Yields 12 bite-sized pieces (1 piece is one serving)

1 cup creamy natural almond butter
1 tsp. organic stevia extract, optional
1 ½ cups unsweetened shredded coconut, divided
1 tsp. vanilla extract
Himalayan sea salt

Combine almond butter, vanilla, stevia, and 1 cup of the shredded coconut in an electric mixer or with a hand mixer. Place mixture in the freezer to let it set. Mix together the rest of the coconut flakes and a pinch of sea salt, and spread onto a plate. Use a tablespoon scooper to scoop out the almond butter mixture into a ball, and roll it in the sea salt and coconut, coating evenly. Serve immediately and store remaining bites in the refrigerator or freezer.

Nutritional Information: Total Calories 181, Total Fat 17g, Carbohydrates 6g, Sugars 2g, Dietary Fiber 2g, Protein 4g, Sodium 98mg, good source of vitamin E

STRAWBERRY SHORTCAKE ICE CREAM BALLS

Yields about 20 ice cream balls (2 ice cream balls is one serving)

8 oz. whole milk ricotta cheese
2 tbsp. raw honey
2 tsp. pure vanilla extract
1 cup fresh organic strawberries
1 cup angel food cake protein powder (vanilla will work also)
8 oz. full-fat cream cheese
1 package natural graham crackers, about 7-8 crackers (no artificial preservatives, flavors, coloring, or high fructose corn syrup)

Combine ricotta, honey, vanilla, cream cheese, strawberries, and protein powder with a mixer. Place in freezer for 2 hours. Crush graham crackers either with a food processor or smash them in a plastic bag. Pour crumbs onto a plate, scoop out the ice cream mixture with a tablespoon scooper and coat each ball with the graham cracker crumbs. Serve immediately. Take leftover ice cream balls and wrap them in wax paper 2 at a time, and place in a plastic bag for an easy snack when you're craving something sweet!

Nutritional Information: Total Calories 245, Total Fat 14g, Carbohydrates 16g, Sugars 9g, Dietary Fiber 2g, Protein 12g, Sodium 280mg, good source of calcium, vitamin A, zinc, and copper

Yields 14 muffins (1 muffin is one serving)

2 cups full-fat cottage cheese
5 egg whites
2 tbsp. cinnamon
3 small red apples, finely chopped
¼ cup chopped walnuts

Preheat oven to 350 degrees. Combine all ingredients in a bowl, mixing well to combine. Spoon into silicon muffin tins or regular muffin tins greased with coconut oil. DO NOT bake these in paper holders. Sprinkle walnuts on tops of muffins and bake for 35 minutes. Cool before serving. Store in refrigerator.

Nutritional Information: Total Calories 64, Total Fat 1g, Carbohydrates 5g, Sugars 3g, Dietary Fiber 1g, Protein 5g, Sodium 129mg

STRAWBERRY CHEESECAKE BITES

Yields 16 servings (1 square is one serving)

15 oz. whole milk ricotta cheese
8 natural graham crackers (no artificial preservatives, flavors, colors, or high fructose corn syrup)
2 tbsp. raw honey
2 tsp. pure vanilla extract
1 pint fresh organic strawberries, sliced

Combine ricotta, honey, and vanilla with a hand mixer. Refrigerate for at least 30 minutes. Break graham crackers in half and spread 1 tbsp. of ricotta mixture on each and top with sliced berries. Sprinkle with stevia if desired.

Nutritional Information: Total Calories 96, Total Fat 4g, Carbohydrates 10g, Sugars 6g, Dietary Fiber 1g, Protein 4g, Sodium 67mg

PUMPKIN PIE BITES

Yields 16 servings (1 square is one serving)

16 oz. plain Greek yogurt (10% milk-fat is best, use 2% at minimum)
15 oz. can pumpkin puree (not pumpkin pie filling)
1 tsp. ground cinnamon
½ tsp. pumpkin pie spice
3 tsp. stevia
8 natural graham crackers (no artificial preservatives, flavors, colors, or high fructose corn syrup)

Mix all ingredients except graham crackers with a hand mixer. Refrigerate for at least 1 hour. Break graham crackers in half and spread 1 tbsp. of pumpkin mixture on each. Sprinkle with pumpkin pie spice and serve.

Nutritional Information: Total Calories 72, Total Fat 3g, Carbohydrates 10g, Sugars 4g, Dietary Fiber 1g, Protein 4g, Sodium 96mg, good source of vitamin A

PUMPKIN CHOCOLATE CHIP COOKIES

Yields 7 servings (2 cookies is one serving)

1 cup raw almond butter
½ cup pumpkin puree (not pumpkin pie filling)
¼ cup pure maple syrup
¾ cup dried apples, chopped, no sugar added
¼ cup dried cranberries, no sugar added
¼ cup shredded unsweetened coconut flakes
¼ cup coconut flour
½ cup dark chocolate chips, at least 60%
2 tsp. pumpkin pie spice
1 tsp. vanilla extract
¼ tsp. sea salt

Preheat the oven to 350 degrees. Mix together the dried apples, dried cranberries, shredded coconut, coconut flour, pumpkin pie spice, sea salt, and chocolate chips, set aside. In another bowl, mix together the pumpkin puree, maple syrup, almond butter, and vanilla extract. Fold the dry ingredients into the wet. Use a tablespoon scooper to place cookies onto parchment lined baking sheet, press down with a fork and bake for 10 minutes. Let cookies cool and store in the refrigerator.

Nutritional Information: Total Calories 476, Total Fat 28g, Carbohydrates 55g, Sugars 35g, Dietary Fiber 9g, Protein 8g, Sodium 64mg

PUMPKIN CHEESECAKE SQUARES

Yields 16 servings (1 square is one serving)

1 cup full-fat greek yogurt (10% is best, use 2% at minimum)
1 15 oz. can pumpkin
15 oz. whole-milk ricotta cheese
1 ½ tbsp. ground cinnamon
1 tsp. pumpkin pie spice
½ tsp. ground ginger
½ tsp. nutmeg
1 tsp. maple extract
1 organic free-range egg
8 natural graham crackers, crushed (no artificial flavors, colors, sweeteners, preservatives, or high fructose corn syrup)
½ cup coconut flour
8 tbsp. grass-fed butter
1 cup chopped pecans

Preheat the oven to 350 degrees. Grind the graham crackers very fine with a food processor or by smashing in a plastic bag. Mix with coconut flour and pour into a 9x13 baking dish. Melt butter and pour over mixture, mixing very well to combine and pressing into the bottom of the dish to form the crust. Bake for 10 minutes. In a large mixing bowl, combine pumpkin, yogurt, ricotta cheese, spices, maple extract, and the egg. Pour on top of crust, top with pecans, and return to the oven for 45 minutes. Remove from oven and let cool. ***Place in refrigerator for 2-4 hours before serving, this dish is best served chilled.***

Nutritional Information: Total Calories 228, Total Fat 19g, Carbohydrates 12g, Sugars 4g, Dietary Fiber 2g, Protein 8g, Sodium 67mg

CHOCOLATE AVOCADO MOUSSE

Yields 4 servings (1/2 cup servings)

2 ripe avocados
½ cup unsweetened full-fat coconut milk
2 scoops grass-fed chocolate whey protein
1 tbsp. cocoa powder
pinch of cinnamon
optional toppings: chopped nuts, fresh berries, dark chocolate shavings, unsweetened shredded coconut

Combine all ingredients in a food processor or blender until creamy. Refrigerate for 2+ hours and serve chilled with desired toppings.

Nutritional Information: Total Calories 213, Total Fat 15g, Carbohydrates 11g, Sugars 2g, Dietary Fiber 6g, Protein 13g, Sodium 35mg, good source of copper, magnesium, vitamin B6, vitamin E, folate, and thiamin

Thank you for purchasing and reading Getting Intimate In The Kitchen. As a thank you, Nutrition Vixen would like to offer you additional **bonus recipes**! Just e-mail support@nutritionvixen.com with the code **VIXEN1** in the subject line to receive your gift!

CONNECT WITH ME:

Website: http://www.nutritionvixen.com
Facebook: http://facebook.com/heatherderanja?fref=ts
Instagram: http://Instagram.com/nutritionvixen
Twitter: http://twitter.com/nutritionvixen

Disclaimer: The views in this book do not necessarily reflect the values, thoughts or opinions of the Academy of Nutrition and Dietetics. Nutrition Vixen's nutrition and lifestyle views and beliefs have been influenced by Heather's education, professional experience as a Registered Dietitian, and evidence-based information. The information and recipes in this book are not meant to diagnose, treat, or cure disease. It is not meant to replace or substitute the recommendations of your physician or health care provider. If you believe you have a medical condition or problem, contact your health care provider.

All recipes indicated as dairy free, gluten free, or egg free (GF, DF, EF), are subject to change based on individual purchase of ingredients and contamination. If you have an allergy or sensitivity to any food or food group, please select ingredients that are free of this substance.

Variations in ingredients, products, and measurements may result in approximate nutritional values. Each analysis is based on ingredients initially listed and does not include optional ingredients, garnishes, fat used to grease pans, or serving suggestions unless noted.